Duct Tape Teambuilding Games

50 Fun Activities To Help Your Team Stick Together

Tom Heck
Teamwork Coach

ISBN 978-1-60743-908-0

Published by Life Coach, Inc.
PO Box 1831
Asheville, NC 28802

Printed in the United States of America
First Edition

Limit of Liability
Disclaimer of Warranty

Dedication

This book is dedicated to my wonderful son Joseph who is one of my favorite teachers. I love you Joseph.

~ Daddy

Acknowledgements

A sincere thank you goes to the amazing students and staff of the Warren Wilson College Outdoor Leadership Program. Their pictures appear throughout this book as a means to help you more fully understand how to play the games,

Warren Wilson College is located near my home in Asheville, North Carolina, USA and I've had the great privilege of working with the staff and students of this great college for many years. This college consistently attracts students who are curious, thoughtful, and engaging and the caring and brilliant staff draw out and nurture the best in them.

Learn more about Warren Wilson College and its Outdoor Leadership Program at the school's website:

www.warren-wilson.edu

I also send a great big thank you to the many people who've taught me how to lead teambuilding games including Karl Rohnke, Jim Cain, Sam Sikes, Chris Cavert, Michelle Cummings, Betsy Hipple, Viva Pizer, Jeff Long, and Earl Davis.

Table of Contents

Introduction

Duct tape has a well-earned reputation for being the ultimate all-purpose fix-it tool. It's been used to make repairs around the home and in the most inhospitable environments including the moon where it was used to repair a fender on the lunar rover during the Apollo 17 mission!

The attributes that make it the world's most reached for repair tool are also the same ones that make it the perfect prop for leading a wide variety of teambuilding games: it's versatile, strong, and flexible (the same traits of highly successful teams!).

This book is filled with fun teambuilding activities for all ages. Some of the games require more brain power than physical effort (and vice versa). Some of the games work well with large groups and others with small groups. While the games are fun to play, they can also help you learn important lessons about how to work successfully together.

To help you learn effectively how to lead these games, I've created a password-protected website that contains video clips of all the 50 Duct Tape Teambuilding Games. You'll find the web address and the login information at the beginning of each game description.

If there was ever a time for people to learn how to work together (and stick together) it's now; so, get yourself a roll of duct tape and start teaching teamwork!

Safety

No single book can substitute for practical experience and education. While this book serves as an introduction to leading teambuilding games, it is only an introduction. Reading this book is no substitute for professional training. The reader is advised to seek out the best possible training in the field of adventure-based experiential education, safety and risk management before attempting any of the activities in this book.

I strongly encourage you to allow the participants to choose their level of challenge. Allow each individual to communicate his or her comfort level with the activity and to join in, rather than be coerced into, participation. Challenge and adventure programs are an opportunity for participants to experience growth, and consequently, they should be the result of an invitation, rather than a requirement.

It's imperative that you know the physical and emotional strengths and limitations of the group you're working with. Don't present an activity that's beyond the physical and/or emotional limitations of your group or any member of your group. If there's any question in your mind as to whether an activity is appropriate for your group - DON'T DO IT! Consult a qualified adventure-based experiential educator.

The Importance of Spotting

Some of the activities presented in this book require the participants to lift each other off the ground. This can be dangerous for both the lifter and the person being lifted. For this reason, you as the leader must be able to convey the importance of proper spotting.

Spotting is the art of protecting a team member's head and upper body from the impact of a fall. Spotting does not mean that you catch a person when he falls. It merely means that you create a cushion, effectively slowing down their fall.

Effective spotting requires that all participants pay close attention to what's going on. If the group or any member of the group is not ready to participate in an activity that requires spotting, choose another activity that doesn't require spotting.

Depending on your group, it may take months to work up to an activity that requires spotting.

To be effective spotters, participants must have a high degree of trust. If participants have been into horseplay or are using language (or other forms of communication) that takes away from the feeling of trust, then you must reconsider any activity that involves spotting.

Spotting is a difficult task to teach as the potential spotter usually doesn't recognize his importance until he actually has to support a falling body. The following are pointers for teaching spotting:

- Explain the concept and meaning of spotting.
- Practice spotting with participants before they actually need to use the skill in an activity.
- Promote the attitude that teasing/joking about not catching someone has no place in your program.
- The activities in this book require a minimum number of 2 spotters and depending on the skill and ability level of your particular group, more spotters may be necessary.
- Supervise spotters closely.
- The leader must model spotting.
- A good spotter shares the responsibility of spotting equally. It is easier and safer to work as a team when spotting.
- Spotters should stand in a balanced position, holding hands up in a "ready position," or as some say "bumpers up". Spotters should focus on the participant.
- Spotters should cushion a fall, not catch and hold, and should move with the direction of force.

Spotting Safety Guidelines_

- Make sure all participants understand the importance of proper spotting prior to starting any activity.

- The activity leader must have a clear understanding of the physical and emotional abilities and limitations of each member of the group prior to starting. This information should be used to determine the appropriateness of a particular activity.

- The leader must participate in spotting - paying close attention to the head, neck and upper back.

- When lifting one of the participants is essential to successfully solve a challenge, the leader must effectively teach participants how to safely lift so that injury is avoided. Remember: lift with your legs, not with your back.

Ain't No Flies

Group Size: 10 - 50 (or more)

Age Range: middle school – adult

Intensity: Mental: easy...♦......................hard

Physical: easy....♦.....................hard

Time: 20 – 40 minutes (without debrief)

Space: minimal..........♦.............lots

Set Up Time: 1 minute

Amount of Duct Tape Required: 10 - 30 feet

View Video: www.DuctTapeTeambuildingGames.com

Username: duct Password: tape

Game Objective

Get the person across from you on your side of the line.

Skills Developed

Creativity, Competition vs. Cooperation mindset, Leadership

Set Up / Preparation

1. Create a line on the ground with duct tape. The line needs to be as long as the group is wide (see below).
2. Divide the group into two halves with the groups standing on opposite sides of the line (facing the line). Each group is two large paces away from the line.
3. Everyone must have a partner and partners should be directly across the line from each other. If you have an odd number of people, then have three people working together.

Presenting the Challenge

1. You (the leader) stand at the end of Line A (side A) and tell the group to repeat what you are about to say: "There ain't no flies on me! (they repeat while pointing at themselves). Then, with a bit more emphasis, "There AIN'T no flies on me!" (they repeat while pointing at themselves). "There might be flies on YOU!" (they repeat while pointing at their partner on the other side of the line). "But there ain't no flies on me!" (they repeat while pointing at themselves). Then you say to Line A "Good job! Now, take one big step forward!" (Line A steps forward toward the line as a group).
2. You then walk over to the other side – Line B – and proceed to repeat the same process with this group, but before you start, you look at them and say "You aren't going to take that are you?" (you're purposefully egging them on just a little). "There ain't no flies on me! (they repeat while pointing at themselves). Then, with a bit more emphasis, "There AIN'T no flies on me!" (they repeat while pointing at themselves). "There might be flies on YOU!" (they repeat while pointing at their partner on the other side of the line). "But there ain't no flies on me!" (they repeat while pointing at themselves). Then you say to Line B "Good job! Now, take one big step forward!" (Line B steps forward toward the line as a group).
3. You then return to repeat the entire process with Line A. Before starting, you attempt to egg on Line A one more time by

saying something like "OK. This is your last chance. Don't take that from them!" When they are done, you have Line A take their final big step up to the line. At this point everyone in Line A is standing with their toes to the line.

4. You then return to Line B for the final time and go through the "Ain't no flies on me" sequence again. Before starting, you attempt to egg on Line A one more time by saying something like "OK. This is your last chance. Don't take that from them!"
5. FINALLY – When both Line A and Line B are facing each other toe-to-toe at the line you quickly announce to the group the following: "Your next set of directions are as follows…as quickly as you can, get the person across from you on your side of the line! Go!" What usually ensues 9 times out of 10 is a tug-o-war pulling session between partners. I let the mayhem (the pulling) go on for about 5 seconds; if you let it go on too long someone might get hurt.

Rules

No rules other than what you found above in the “Presenting the Challenge” section.

Safety Warning

1. Have the participants remove rings, watches and bracelets before this activity because people will inevitably start pulling each other by the wrists which may cause damage to valuables.
2. If you have participants with weak or injured backs, necks, shoulders, arms, etc. do not choose this activity.
3. Everyone must be wearing shoes and preferably tennis or basketball shoes.

Facilitator Notes

1. It’s hard to find an activity that produces a more dramatic effect than this one especially with regard to pointing out the effects of lose-lose and win-lose thinking (as opposed to win-win thinking).

2. With a group of 30 people doing this activity (15 on either side of the line), there is usually one pair that doesn't end up pulling and tugging on each other. Pulling and tugging is almost always what I see when I lead this activity. The surprising thing is that pulling and tugging is not necessary to "win".
3. There are really two activities happening here. The first is the "set up" where I'm getting people riled up with the whole "ain't no flies" thing. I use this as a build up to the final set of instructions which are as follows: "Your next set of directions are as follows…as quickly as you can, get the person across from you on your side of the line! Go!" As I said, the normal reaction to this set of directions is to pull one's partner onto one's side of the line, which creates a win – lose scenario (the winner being the one who successfully pulled his partner onto his side).
4. There is a win – win scenario: the partners calmly step over the line simultaneously. Remember the directions? To win, all that must happen is for my partner to cross over to MY side of the line. It doesn't matter where I'm standing in order for me to win. This realization rarely happens in the "heat of battle."
5. Now about this "set up" issue. Yes – I do purposely attempt to get the two lines agitated with the whole "ain't no flies" thing. I propose that life "sets us up" on a daily basis. You make the determination…Are the following situations "set ups" for confrontation and win – lose scenarios? Palestinians v. Israelis; Black vs. White; Muslim vs. Christian; Male vs. Female; Wealthy vs. Poor; Democrats vs. Republicans.
6. Sometimes people finish this activity and are a bit embarrassed at how they reacted, wishing they had recognized the situation immediately as an opportunity to practice win – win. What I offer to the group is that we as a culture (in the US) see and experience win – lose and lose – lose way more frequently than win – win. All it takes is turning on the television or opening a newspaper and trying to look for win – win described in the major media (it's hard to find). I suggest that looking for win – win requires a conscious effort, at least at first.
7. I once led this activity with a group of 200 classroom teachers. I had 100 on one side of a very long line and 100 on the other side. Though this did work, I recommend breaking a group

this size into smaller groups of 50 (25 on each side of the line) this requires large space and multiple lines on the ground.

Debriefing Suggestions

1. Upon calling "Time out!" to end the activity, I ask people to form into discussion groups of 3 or 4. I then pose this question to the small discussion groups:
2. "I'd like you to discuss the three major types of interactions we have with each other: (1) win-lose, (2) lose-lose, (3) win-win. Describe the type of interaction you just experienced and determine why it happened the way it did."
3. Each small group then has a discussion. I allow approximately 5-7 minutes and then have the entire group gather together to share their findings.
4. During this large group meeting, my goal is for the group to reveal (share) the truths about win-lose and lose-lose behaviors. We talk about how easy it is to slip into this type of behavior and how we must be diligent when looking for win-win opportunities because they are everywhere.

Variations

Instead of a line, you can create a circle on the ground which would require one group to start on the inside of the circle and the other group on the outside.

History

I learned this activity from master facilitator Earl Davis **www.moonshadow.net**

Related Quote

"Things won are done; joy's soul lies in the doing."

~ William Shakespeare

All Aboard

Group Size: 8 – 12
Age Range: elementary – adult
Intensity: Mental: easy............ ♦..... ....hard
Physical: easy...................... ♦...hard
Time: 5 – 30 minutes (without debrief)
Space: minimal....... ♦..................lots
Set Up Time: 2 minutes
Amount of Duct Tape Required: 10 - 15 feet
View Video: www.DuctTapeTeambuildingGames.com
Username: duct Password: tape

Objective

The entire group must fit in the square.

Skills Developed

Problem Solving, Trust, Planning, Resource Management

Set Up / Preparation

Create a large square on the ground using duct tape measuring 2 ft x 2 ft.

Presenting the Challenge

1. Ask the team to gather around the square taped to the ground.
2. Presentation Script: "Your challenge is to get your entire team inside this square. You must follow and obey the rules throughout the game." [read the rules below]

Rules

1. Everyone must be touching the ground inside the square with at least one foot (or part of your foot).
2. You may not touch the ground located outside the square. You can touch the square itself (duct tape).
3. The square (duct tape) may not be moved or rearranged.
4. The group must stay on/in the square for the length of time it takes them to sing one round of "Row, Row, Row Your Boat" (or the song of your choice).
5. During the song, no one can touch the ground outside the square. Should anyone violate this rule, the entire group must retry that attempt.

Safety Warning

1. Don't allow participants to pile up or get on each other's backs or shoulders. These methods usually result in injury.
2. Counsel the group not to fall on top of anyone.
3. Always spot the group, making sure to prevent head, neck and back injuries.
4. No locking of elbows.
5. No standing on other people's feet.

6. Closed toed shoes must be worn at all times (no bare feet, no sandals, etc. allowed - this is for safety reasons).

Story Line

"Your team is on a sinking ship. The good news is that a rescue ship is coming. The bad news is that the water is infested with hungry sharks. Your team must stand on top of the last remaining part of the boat that's still sticking out of the water. If you can stay out of the water as a team (the length of the song "Row, Row, Row Your Boat") then the sharks will leave."

Facilitator Notes

1. The square measuring 2 feet x 2 feet can hold 15 adults who are working really well together (it's hard but it can be done).
2. If the group quickly solves this challenge you might want to give them a harder version - make a smaller square (18 inches x 18 inches).
3. If the group is having real difficulty, consider adding a smaller square next to the larger square to give the team a little extra room to stand.
4. It's common for younger age participants to fall to the ground (sometimes with a bit of dramatic flair) while doing this activity. Be aware of this and make sure people don't fall on top of each other.

Debriefing Suggestions

1. If the group has an easy time solving the challenge with a larger square, I'll create smaller and smaller squares (making the challenge harder and harder). As the size of the square gets smaller, the group usually goes through a period where they don't believe they can fit in such a small area ("This is impossible!"). It's only through creative thinking and hard work that the group is able to solve this challenge.
2. I like to use this activity to lead into a discussion about what's "impossible". When something is viewed as impossible, it's usually because of the limiting beliefs someone holds. An example of this might include beliefs from several centuries ago that held the world is flat. Another might include the old

belief that the earth is the center of the universe. If you were to tell someone during the early 1800's that people would be able to communicate with each other around the world instantaneously (telephone) or that we will fly to the moon and come back, you would have been laughed at. Quite often, the only thing that limits us is our beliefs. If a person believes something is possible, he will take different action than if he believes it is impossible.

3. What did the group have to believe in order to be successful?
4. This is a great activity to discuss the concept of failure. If the group is able to solve the challenge using a larger square I'll give them a smaller and smaller square to solve. The group will get to a point where the challenge is greater than their ability to solve it in the given amount of time. I will ask if their inability to solve it means they're a failure. You'll find that some people in the group have rules for themselves that make failure easy to achieve ("In order for me to fail, all I have to know is that I didn't complete a given task.").
5. Others in the group will have rules that make failure hard to experience ("In order for me to fail, I must not learn anything. As long as I learn something, I have succeeded.")
6. Which rules about failure serve you best?
7. Interesting point: Babe Ruth, the famous baseball home run hitter and hall of famer also held a record for having the most strike outs in a season.

Variations

1. As previously mentioned, provide the group with a large, easy to stand in, square. Then progressively make the square smaller and smaller (making the challenge harder and harder). Provide all three platforms for the group to stand on when you start out.
2. Provide the group with a (relatively) small square to begin with. Use your best judgment here. Pick a size you know they can do and a size that will challenge them at the same time.

History

Karl Rohnke provided a description of this activity in his book "Silver Bullets" published in 1984. **www.karlrohnke.com**

Related Quote

"A round man cannot be expected to fit in a square hole right away. He must have time to modify his shape." **~ Mark Twain**

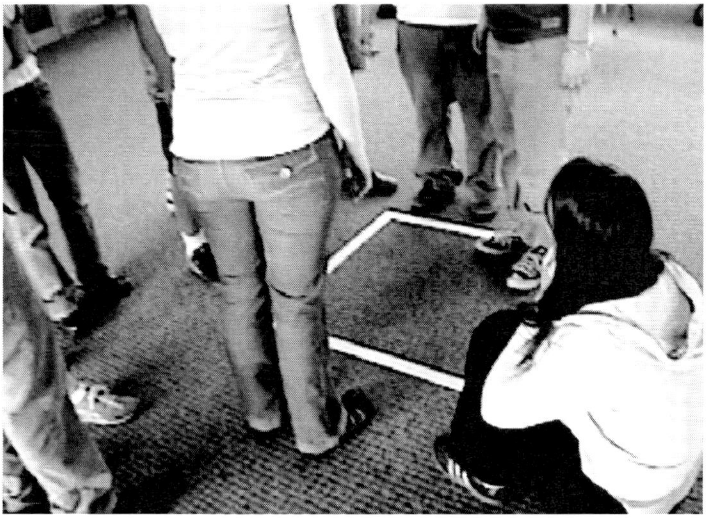

All My Neighbors

Group Size: 10 - 30

Age Range: middle school – adult

Intensity: Mental: easy...♦......................hard

Physical: easy....♦.....................hard

Time: 5 minutes (without debrief)

Space: minimal...........♦..............lots

Set Up Time: 1 minute

Amount of Duct Tape Required: 2 feet

View Video: www.DuctTapeTeambuildingGames.com

Username: duct Password: tape

Game Objective

Share information about yourself in a funny, non-threatening way.

Skills Developed

Communication, Trust, Fun

Set Up / Preparation

1. Have the group stand in a circle with arms stretched out to sides (forming a letter "T") - finger tips should almost touch their partner's on either side.
2. Hand each person a two inch long piece of duct tape and then have everyone stick the duct tape to the ground directly in front of them - this marks a "space" (or "spot").
3. The leader (you, the facilitator) stands in the center of the circle. The leader does not have a spot (piece of duct tape).

Presenting the Challenge

1. The leader (you, the facilitator) stands in the center of the circle. The leader does not have a spot (piece of duct tape). The rest of the group is facing you (the center of the circle).
2. The leader then says something true about them and if the statement is true for anyone standing in the circle, he or she must move to another spot. Because there is one spot less marker than there are people, someone will always be "caught" in the center (after the person in the center makes the true statement they quickly try to find a free spot marker). If you're wondering why this activity is called "All My Neighbors" here's the reason: the person caught in the center says "All my neighbors who love ice cream" or "All my neighbors who've received a speeding ticket", etc.
3. Presentation Script: "I'm about to say something true about myself and if the statement is also true for you or anyone else, you must move to another spot. Because there is one spot marker less than there are people, someone will always be "caught" in the center and this person is our new leader. The new leader will then say something true about him and if it's also true about you, then you'll need to find a new spot. If you end up as a leader, you must start your statement with "All my neighbors who...". Example 1: "All my neighbors who love ice cream". Example 2: "All my neighbors who've received a speeding ticket", etc.

Rules

1. You can't move to an open spot next to you.
2. No running (quick walking is OK).
3. If someone gets "stuck" in the center and doesn't want to be the leader, he/she can choose to decline the opportunity and select a volunteer to be the leader for that round.

Safety Warning

1. Energetic participants can tend to move too quickly in this game (even run) and this is not safe. Everyone must walk to help prevent collisions.
2. Be careful about leading this game on slick surfaces.

Story Line

"While visiting a foreign land, your team is introduced to a new way for people to learn about each other. Since you want to be polite you all decide to join in the fun."

Facilitator Notes

1. I've led this activity with all kinds of groups, both young and old, and it's always fun. With younger groups you might find that they will purposely try to get "caught" in the middle just so they can have a chance of being the leader.
2. I've seen this done with groups larger than 30, but it seems to lose a part of the excitement. If your group is larger than 30, consider dividing the group into small groups of 15 – 20 and have them work separately.
3. One of the things I like about this activity is that you can participate without participating. By this I mean if someone doesn't want to divulge something about himself (and so do not move to a new spot) he can stay put. This gives people the option of participating at the level they choose.
4. Sometimes I'll ask a group to keep the truths they share "G rated" (as in the movie rating). I'll do this if I sense the group might say something inappropriate.

Debriefing Suggestions

I usually don't debrief this activity. I use it as a funny and fast get-to-know-you game. If I do debrief it at all I might ask: "What did you like about how this group played that game? Did you see any behavior you'd like to see the group repeat in the next activity?"

Variations

Instead of playing as individuals, have everyone partner up. Even the "leader" is a pair working together. Instead of one person standing behind one spot marker, a pair (team) stands behind a spot marker. The leader (pair) must find something that is true about the two of them and then announce it. Pairs can only move if it's also true about BOTH of them.

History

I learned this game from master teamwork coach Betsy Hipple.

Related Quote

"Today we know that all living beings who strive to maintain life and who long to be spared pain - all living beings on earth are our neighbors" ***~ Albert Schweitzer***

Amoeba Electric Fence

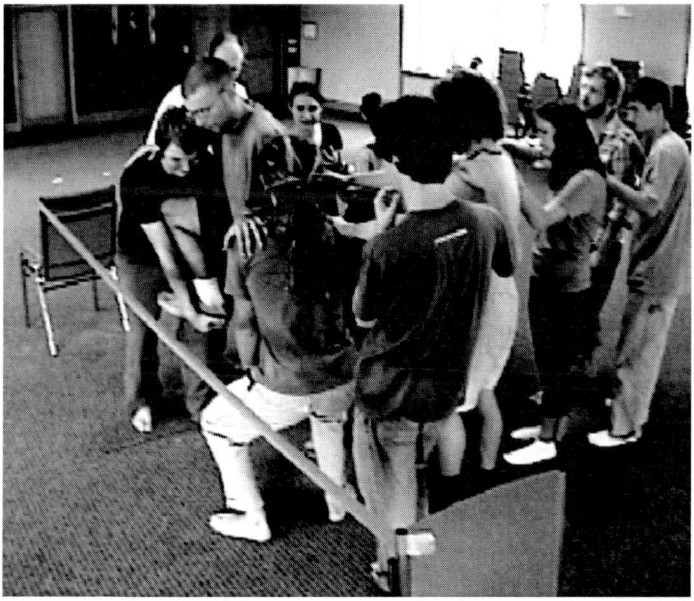

Group Size: 4 – 15
Age Range: high school – adult
Intensity: Mental: easy.........♦................hard
Physical: easy....................♦.....hard
Time: 15 – 40 minutes (without debrief)
Space: minimal...........♦..............lots
Set Up Time: 3 minutes
Amount of Duct Tape Required: 10 - 15 feet
View Video: www.DuctTapeTeambuildingGames.com
Username: duct Password: tape

Game Objective

The entire team must cross over the top of the "electric fence".

Skills Developed

Trust, Planning, Problem Solving, Roles and Responsibilities

Set Up / Preparation

1. Create a clear playing area. The space must be free from any obstacles that may endanger the group while playing the game.
2. Create the "electric fence" by using a long section (10 - 15 feet) of duct tape to create a line parallel to the ground. You can do this by attaching the ends of the duct tape to two chairs that are some distance apart. Or attach one end of the duct tape to a wall and the other end to a desk. The higher the duct tape is off the ground the more challenging the game will be. I recommend placing the duct tape no higher than the average of the group's pants inseam. For safety reasons, don't make the line higher than 4 feet.

Presenting the Challenge

1. Gather the group on one side of the "electric fence".
2. Presentation Script: "This duct tape represents an imaginary electric fence. Your challenge is to travel from the side of the electric fence you're on now over to the other side of the electric fence. Here are the rules you must follow throughout the game." [read the rules below]

Rules

1. The electric fence, as it is presented at the beginning of the activity, may not be altered.
2. The electric fence may not be touched by anything (skin, hair, clothing, etc.)
3. The group may not utilize the space directly under the electric fence. Think of this space as having an ultra-thin and impenetrable force field.
4. All members of the team must remain in contact with each other at all times throughout the game (regardless of what side of the electric fence you're on). The group must act as ONE "amoeba". It would be a rule violation if, for example, three people are in physical contact with each other but not in contact with the rest of the larger group.

5. Team members are allowed to reposition themselves as long as they ALWAYS stay in physical contact with the group.
6. No launching or throwing of team members over the electric fence. Travel over the fence must be done in a safe way.
7. No other supplies may be used in this activity.
8. Violation of a rule may result in a penalty (example: starting all over again).

Safety Warning

1. Because this game involves lifting, it's important to teach proper spotting techniques prior to giving the group this challenge.
2. Do not allow participants to hit their heads or spines on the ground. This is very important. Since people will be lifted over the fence by their teammates, it's ideal to have cushions/pads placed under the horizontal bar of the fence. This will help minimize the effect of a fall should one occur.
3. If your group is not strong enough (physically), mature enough and/or calm enough, do not attempt this activity.
4. People with knee, ankle or back injuries or problems should not participate.

Story Line

"Traveling through the land of Goop, your team has mysteriously been turned into an amoeba (single cell organism). Though it's somewhat funny and entertaining to be an amoeba, it will make it impossible to return home and live a normal life. Therefore, your team must cross over a magical barrier (duct tape) to change back to your normal selves. Don't touch the magic barrier!"

Facilitator Notes

1. A high degree of trust is required to successfully accomplish this challenge. This challenge is best for a group that is fairly advanced as far as maturity and their ability to safely care for each other are concerned.
2. As the facilitator, be ready to help spot the group members during the game. If team members aren't taking the safety of teammates seriously then stop the game immediately.

3. Consider presenting this activity in stages. First set up the electric fence height low so that the group can easily travel over the electric fence. Then continue to increase the height of the electric fence.

Debriefing Suggestions

Prior to starting the activity, ask the group to identify some of the obstacles (hurdles, “fences”) that stand between them and their goals. Suggest to the group that the electric fence represents these obstacles.

Variations

1. Supply the group with a “life line” made out of 10-20 feet of duct tape (sticky side folded in on itself). Instead of requiring the group to stay in contact with each other, require the group to stay in contact with the “life line” throughout the game.
2. Divide the group in half. Have the groups start on opposite sides of the electric fence. The groups must switch sides. Will the two groups cooperate? (I hope so!).

History

A variation of this activity was first documented in “Silver Bullets” by Karl Rohnke **www.karlrohnke.com**

Related Quote

“Fences are made for those who cannot fly.” **~ Elbert Hubbard**

Learn how to help your team move as one in my Manager As Coach Boot Camp.
www.ManagerAsCoachBootCamp.com

Balance Tug

Group Size: 2 – 16

Age Range: elementary school – adult

Intensity: Mental: easy....♦......................hard

Physical: easy................♦.........hard

Time: 5 – 10 minutes (without debrief)

Space: minimal............♦.............lots

Set Up Time: 1 minute

Amount of Duct Tape Required: 60 - 70 feet

View Video: www.DuctTapeTeambuildingGames.com

Username: duct Password: tape

Game Objective

Beat your opponent by either making him lose his balance or take all of his duct tape.

Skills Developed

Fun, Energizer

Set Up / Preparation

Create a 15-feet long section of duct tape "rope". It takes three people to create this duct tape rope: one person who dispenses the duct tape and two people to hold the ends of the duct tape. Pull off a 15-foot section of duct tape and have two volunteers hold the ends of this piece of duct tape. Repeat this process three more times, allowing all four long pieces of duct tape to stick to each other. Now have the duct tape holders twist the duct tape rope (the four "strands") - this will help bind the four 15-feet long strips of duct tape together to make one duct tape rope. If you can, try to string out the 15-feet long strips of duct tape so they sticky sides are not exposed (this isn't critical). NOTE: This is the same duct tape rope that is used in Balance Tug, Turnstile, Jump Rope Record, Throw Up, and Yurt Circle.

Presenting the Challenge

1. This is an activity for two people and it's competitive in nature. Two people face each other with about 5 feet of space between them. Each person must stand with his or her feet side by side, then squat down.
2. Have each person grab onto the duct tape rope with an equal amount of extra rope behind or to the side of them. When you say go, each person attempts to win by getting the other to lose his/her balance (move feet, cause him to put a hand down, stand up, etc.) or pull all of the duct tape rope away from the other person.
3. <u>Presentation Script:</u> "This game is simple. Try to win by either (a) pulling all of your opponent's duct tape rope away or (b) causing your opponent to lose his/her balance." [read the rules below]

Rules

1. Each person must start off with equal amounts of duct tape rope.

2. Do not allow participants to wrap the duct tape rope around their hands, arms or bodies as this could result in injury.
3. The feet must be side by side with the insides of the feet touching each another.

Safety Warning

1. Use high quality (expensive and thick) duct tape to make the duct tape rope.
2. People with knee, back or shoulder injuries should not play this game.

Story Line

"Two people carefully balanced on the top of telephone polls which are standing in gooey mud. Whoever loses his or her balance falls into the mud!"

Facilitator Notes

1. This activity seems dependent on brute force whereas it's actually about strategy. Often an opponent can be beat simply by letting the webbing slide through the hands allowing the opponent to fall backwards.
2. A small person can beat a much larger person. This is not a game of tug-of-war though some think that pulling really hard is the best strategy.
3. Sometimes when I'm working with a new group of kids, I'll use this activity as a warm up to break the ice and have fun. I playfully present the challenge and then watch what happens. Are people eager to get up and play or are they reserved and watchful?
4. Recycle the duct tape rope and use it for other games in this book including Yurt Circle, Jump Rope Record, and Turnstile.

Debriefing Suggestions

This activity lends itself to discussions involving balance.

Who do you know that seems to have his or her life in balance? How do you think they do it?

What aspect of your life seems to be in balance? What aspect of your life seems to be out of balance?

If you're out of balance and you want to get back into balance, how do you do it?

Variations

Close your eyes while playing.

History

Karl Rohnke described a variation of this game in one of his fantastic teambuilding games books (he called it "Hunker Hawser"). **www.karlrohnke.com**

Related Quote

"The most important human endeavor is the striving for morality in our actions. Our inner balance and even our very existence depend on it. Only morality in our actions can give beauty and dignity to life." **~ Albert Einstein**

Bus Stop

Group Size: 4 - 40

Age Range: elementary school – adult

Intensity: Mental: easy....♦.....................hard

Physical: easy....♦.....................hard

Time: 5 – 10 minutes (without debrief)

Space: minimal.........♦................lots

Set Up Time: 1 minute

Amount of Duct Tape Required: 20 feet

View Video: www.DuctTapeTeambuildingGames.com

Username: duct Password: tape

Game Objective

Learn more about team members by expressing opinions in front of each other.

Skills Developed

Trust, Fun, Know Others Better

Set Up / Preparation

Using the duct tape, create two parallel lines on the ground - these are the sides of your imaginary bus. The space between the lines should be approximately 15 - 20 feet.

Presenting the Challenge

1. The facilitator stands at one end of the "bus" (at the end of and between the parallel lines.
2. The group stands between the two parallel lines and faces the facilitator (aka "bus driver").
3. The facilitator reads word pairs to the group (see suggested word pairs below). When you (the facilitator) read the first word in the word pair, you will point to your right (to the right side of the bus). When you read the second word in the word pair you'll point to your left (to the left side of the bus). The participants (passengers) must now make a decision and walk across the line on the ground to the word / side they most relate to in this moment. Participants make their decisions independently from each other. For example, the bus driver says "TALK (pointing to the right) and LISTEN (pointing to the left) and the participants walk across the line to the side they like most at this time.
4. Ask everyone to take a quick look at who ended up on their side AND the other side and then say "Everyone back on the bus!" which means everyone is to walk back between the two parallel lines and get ready to listen for the next word pair.
5. The next word pair is given and the participants (passengers) make their selections. The process is repeated several times.
6. <u>Presentation Script:</u> "You are now on an imaginary bus and I'm your bus driver. In a moment I'm going to announce a word pair and then ask you to exit the bus and move toward the word that you most associate with in this moment. We'll play a couple of rounds. Pay attention to the choices people make." [read the rules below]

Suggested Word Pairs

Day Time --- Night Time
Spend Money -- Save Money
Shark --- Dolphin
Chocolate Cake --- Chocolate Ice Cream
Run --- Walk
One Friend --- Many Friends
Triangle --- Square
Deep Sea Diving --- Sky Diving
Something New --- Something Old
Art Class -- Math Class
Little Kid --- Big Kid
Talk --- Listen
Yesterday --- Tomorrow
Problem Solver --- Problem Maker

Rules

Passengers must get off the bus (make a choice) after the bus driver (facilitator) announces a word pair. They must make a choice.

Safety Warning

Keep all wild and dangerous animals away from the playing area.

Story Line

"Your team is on a journey and every great journey involves working together and overcoming challenges. To prepare for the inevitable challenges you will face as a team, it's important for us all to learn more about each other. To facilitate greater understanding, you will take a journey together on an imaginary bus and I (the facilitator) will be your bus driver. During the journey we will make multiple stops and I'll ask you to make a decision as to which side of the bus you'll exit - the side you exit will help the team learn more about you."

Facilitator Notes

1. This activity is best left for groups that are patient. Do not attempt this activity with a rambunctious hyperactive group.
2. The group movement will remind you of a centipede.
3. This activity emphasizes communication, careful steady movement and team coordination.
4. Just for fun, play the sound track of the movie "2001 A Space Odyssey" while the group travels from one spaceship to the other.

Debriefing Suggestions

I use this activity to lead into a discussion about the power of making a real choice. I believe that great teams do not achieve success (consistently) through luck. Long-term success is achieved through the choices we make both as individuals and as a team. Sometimes we make choices consciously and sometimes we make choices without much thought at all. The choices we make on a daily basis create what is known as destiny. By becoming aware of our choices, we can decide whether they serve us or not. Each choice we make leads us either closer to or farther from our life's mission or purpose.

Variations

Have participants think of word pairs that would challenge the group and then take over as the bus driver.

History

This game was taught to me by master teambuilder Jeff Long.

Related Quote

"There is no value in life except what you choose to place upon it and no happiness in any place except what you bring to it yourself." **~ Henry David Thoreau**

Caterpillar Traverse

Group Size: 4 – 10

Age Range: elementary school – adult

Intensity: Mental: easy.........♦................hard

Physical: easy........♦.................hard

Time: 10 – 30 minutes (without debrief)

Space: minimal..................♦......lots

Set Up Time: 5 minutes

Amount of Duct Tape Required: 40 - 50 feet

View Video: www.DuctTapeTeambuildingGames.com

Username: duct Password: tape

Game Objective

With ankles taped, the team travels as a unit from Point A to Point B.

Skills Developed

Clear Communication, Trust, Planning, Patience, Goal Setting and Achievement, Resource Management

Set Up / Preparation

1. Tape two parallel lines (boundary lines) on the ground 9 - 10 feet apart.
2. In between the parallel lines, tape three squares on the ground with sides of the squares measuring approximately two feet. The squares can be placed in a straight line or in a zig-zag manner (see photo). The squares should be no more than 12 inches away from each other and the end squares no more than 12 inches from the parallel lines.

Presenting the Challenge

1. Ask the group to stand behind one of the boundary lines.
2. Have the team line up shoulder to shoulder (and ankle to ankle). Provide each person with a piece of tape long enough to tape their feet (or ankles) to their neighbor's. When that is done, the entire team will be standing shoulder to shoulder with feet (or ankles) taped together. NOTE: Do not tape skin. Be aware that duct tape may damage some types of shoes and clothing.
3. Presentation Script: "Your challenge is to travel from the line you're now behind (the starting position) over to and across the other (parallel) line. You must follow and obey the rules throughout the game." [read the rules below]

Rules

1. The tape stuck to the ground must not be moved.
2. The group must remain in a line with feet (or ankles) taped throughout the activity.
3. You cannot step on the ground between the two parallel lines. EXCEPTION: you may step on or inside the squares taped to the ground.
4. No other equipment may be used.

5. Violation of a rule may result in a penalty. (For example: touches between the two parallel lines and outside of the squares may require the team to start over)

Safety Warning

1. People with knee, ankle or back injuries should not participate.
2. Ankles should be taped together loosely to help reduce the likelihood of injuries.
3. It's important for the group to move slowly so that no one gets hurt.
4. Do not allow people to put tape on bare skin because removing the tape will cause injury.

Story Line

"The spacecraft you're currently on has lost all power and will soon begin descending into the Earth's atmosphere (not good). Another spacecraft has been sent to rescue your team. Get your team to the rescue ship before time runs out. Due to the extreme solar wind situation, your team must travel as a unit, staying connected and utilizing the spaceman stepping stones (taped squares on the ground)."

Facilitator Notes

1. This activity is best for groups that are patient. Do not attempt this activity with a rambunctious hyperactive group.
2. The group movement will remind you of a centipede.
3. This activity emphasizes communication, careful steady movement and team coordination.
4. Just for fun, play the sound track of the movie "2001 A Space Odyssey" while the group travels from one spaceship to the other.

Debriefing Suggestions

1. Prior to starting the activity, have the group identify the current situation (spaceship) they are leaving behind - metaphorically this ship represents all that they no longer need and/or those

things that no longer serve them. Also identify the new destination ("rescue ship") and it's qualities.

2. What do the squares on the ground represent?
3. What does the tape around the ankles represent?

Variations

1. Supply the group with a limited amount of time to complete the task (example: 20 minutes).
2. Require two or three people to close their eyes for a part of or all of the activity.
3. Divide the team in half. One group starts on one side and the second starts on the other. The groups must switch places before time runs out. Will they work together or against each other?
4. Do this activity in a room where you can turn the lights off so as to make it completely dark (the facilitator has a flash light to look for rule violations). Warn the group that you might turn the lights off during the activity. If you do turn the lights off, keep them off for a short time (5 to 10 seconds).

History

This game was taught to me by an intern when I worked for the YMCA.

Related Quote

What the caterpillar calls the end of the world, the master calls a butterfly. ~ **Richard Bach**

Channels

Group Size: 4 – 20
Age Range: elementary school – adult
Intensity: <u>Mental</u>: easy.......♦..................hard
<u>Physical</u>: easy........♦.................hard
Time: 10 – 30 minutes (without debrief)
Space: minimal............♦.............lots
Set Up Time: 3 minutes (not including prop creation)
Amount of Duct Tape Required: 40 - 50 feet
View Video: www.DuctTapeTeambuildingGames.com
Username: duct Password: tape

Game Objective

Transport the supplied duct tape balls from Point A to Point B using the duct tape channels (gutters).

Skills Developed

Clear Communication, Planning, Resource Management, Problem Solving

Set Up / Preparation

1. Using duct tape, create four marble size balls. Start by tearing off a 12 inch long piece of duct tape and then ripping lengthwise 4 thin equal width strips. Similar to how you might start a ball of yarn, use one of the thin strips to start your ball -- fold a small portion of the duct tape over and over very tightly. Keep turning and twisting the duct tape ball to keep it spherical. Add thin strips of duct tape as needed. The tighter the ball of duct tape is the easier it will roll (that's good).
2. Using duct tape create a channel (or gutter) for each participant (or have the participants do it). Each channel will require four strips of duct tape 16 inches long. Strips 1 and 2 will be placed on top of each other (sticky sides together). Next, you'll stick strip 3 onto strips 1 and 2; however, strip 3 will overlap strips 1 and 2 by only 3/4 inch lengthwise. Stick strip 4 on to strip 3 (sticky sides together). Like strip 3, strip 4 will overlap strip 1 and 2 by 3/4 inches. Following these directions will result in a rectangle measuring approximately 16 inches x 3 3/4 inches.
3. Attach a 12 inch long piece of duct tape to a vertical surface (wall or chair) about 3 feet off the ground. Be sure to make the sticky side face out. The team will be transporting the duct tape balls onto this piece of duct tape (the balls will stick to the duct tape).

Presenting the Challenge

1. Supply each participant with one channel. Each person holds the channel with two hands and in such a way as to create a gutter effect which allows the duct tape balls to roll down the center of this duct tape channel.
2. Participants position themselves in such a way as to line up all the channels - - if water were to be poured in the first channel it would run along through all the channels.
3. The distance the group must transport the four duct tape balls is greater than the distance of all the channels combined (end

to end). That means, in order to complete the challenge, the group will have to "leap frog" as the duct tape balls roll through the channels. It is this leap frog effect that poses such a challenge for the team and that is what makes this game so much fun.

4. Presentation Script: "Your challenge is to transport the four supplied balls made from duct tape from Point A to Point B (the strip of duct tape hanging on the wall). You must follow all the rules." [read the rules below]

Rules

1. The duct tape balls may not touch anything other than the channels and the piece of duct tape at the end.
2. When there is a duct tape ball in your channel, your feet must be planted and stationary.
3. Channels/people may move when a ball is not in their channel.
4. You may not physically touch another person's channel (but channels may touch each other).
5. Duct tape balls may only move in a forward direction, never backwards.
6. Forward motion of the duct tape balls may not be stopped.
7. Channels must always be in the air (they may not be laid on the ground, floor, table, chairs, etc.).
8. Duct tape balls may not be touched (except to start or restart).
9. Violation of a rule may result in a penalty.

Safety Warning

1. Keep the small duct tape balls away from small children because they're a choking hazard.
2. Make sure the playing area is free of obstacles because when the team is playing this game they may lose track of the surrounding environment.

Story Line

"It seems an animal has stolen four tiny duct tape eggs from an endangered duct tape nest. The mother duct tape roll is frantically looking for her four eggs. If the eggs aren't returned soon the little rolls of duct tape inside the eggs will tragically turn into scotch tape. Your team must transport the tiny duct tape eggs back to the nest (strip of duct tape) before time runs out. Everyone knows duct tape eggs may not be handled by humans while in this stage of development. Therefore, your team is supplied with duct tape egg transportation channels."

Facilitator Notes

Because you placed the strip of duct tape (final destination for the four duct tape balls) farther than the total distance of all of the channels combined, the group will have to "leap frog" to make the duct tape balls stay in the channels. Groups that rush can have an extremely difficult time with this activity.

Debriefing Suggestions

1. I like to use this activity to bring up discussions around the topic/concept of "flow" (flow of ideas, money, resources, etc.). You could ask questions such as "How did this activity mimic the flow of ideas in your organization?" or "If the duct tape balls represented your most important asset, describe how you took care of them."
2. This activity also lends itself well to the topic of goal achievement if the duct tape strip (final destination) were to represent the goal and if the duct tape balls attached to the

duct tape strip mean achievement of the goal. Possible debrief question: How defined are your goals in the real world?

Variations

1. To make this activity easier, remove rule #5 and/or #6 and/or #7.
2. To make this more difficult, have the group transport the duct tape balls up hill (up a staircase) or under/over an obstacle such as a desk, tree, etc.
3. To make this more difficult prohibit any verbal communication in the group.
4. If you don't want to make duct tape balls you can use marbles instead.

History

This game was taught to me by master teambuilder Viva Pizer.

Related Quote

"It is a process of diverting one's scattered forces into one powerful channel." ***~ James Allen***

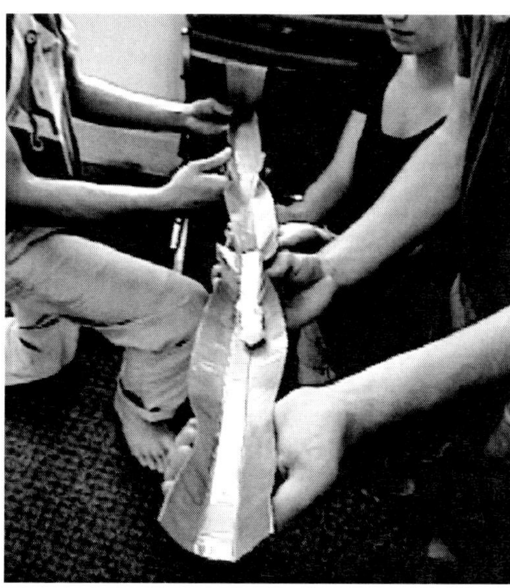

Circle Pass

Group Size: 6 – 15
Age Range: elementary school – adult
Intensity: Mental: easy....♦......................hard
Physical: easy..........♦...............hard
Time: 5 – 10 minutes (without debrief)
Space: minimal.........♦................lots
Set Up Time: 1 minute (not including prop creation)
Amount of Duct Tape Required: 40 - 50 feet
View Video: www.DuctTapeTeambuildingGames.com
Username: duct Password: tape

Game Objective

Pass the duct tape circle (loop) around the circle of people as quickly as possible.

Skills Developed

Goal Setting, Process Improvement, Creativity, Fun

Set Up / Preparation

Create a circle or loop out of an 8 feet long piece of duct tape. As you pull off the 8 feet of duct tape from the roll, fold the sticky side of the duct tape in half lengthwise. Use a short piece of duct tape to join the ends of the 8 feet section.

Presenting the Challenge

1. Ask the group to stand in a circle and hold hands. Then have one pair of people disconnect hands and then reach through the center of the duct tape circle (loop) and rejoin hands. The duct tape circle should now be resting on the joined hands of one pair of people - this is the start/stop "line" for the game.
2. Presentation Script: "Your challenge is to move the duct tape circle (loop) around the circle of people as fast as you can." [read the rules below]

Rules

1. The duct tape circle must travel in a clockwise direction.
2. No letting go of hands.
3. Team members must remain in their respective location (i.e. team members may not walk around).

Safety Warning

1. People with shoulder or neck injuries should not participate.
2. Remove glasses prior to playing (they might fall off and break).
3. Participants must wear flat shoes (no heels).

Story Line

"While traveling through time, your team encounters a rare time loop (aka "duct tape circle"). To continue moving through time and get to your final destination, your team must travel through the time loop as quickly as possible. Remember, don't let go of your hands or someone could go floating off into space."

Facilitator Notes

1. Initially a younger group may find this challenge impossible or at least confusing. They might say "How do you pass the duct tape circle around the circle without letting go of hands?"
2. This activity will invariably get a group laughing as they watch each person pass through the loop.
3. This is not a good activity for people who are obese or who have difficulty balancing.

Debriefing Suggestions

The duct tape circle (loop) in this activity could metaphorically represent a hoop or hoops people jump through on a regular basis (for one reason or another). What are actual hoops in your life that you have jumped through? Are hoops good or bad? Do some people have more to deal with than others? If so, why? What hoops would you add/remove to your life if you could?

Variations

1. Make 2 duct tape circles and require the group to pass both around the circle simultaneously - one in a clockwise direction and the other in a counterclockwise direction.
2. Time the group as they pass the duct tape circle to see how long it takes them to get it all the way around. Allow another attempt to break that record.

History

This game was taught to me by master teambuilder Betsy Hipple.

Related Quote

"It's the circle of life, and it moves us all, through despair and hope, through faith and love, 'till we find our place, on the path unwinding" **~ Elton John**

Consensus Loops

Group Size: 2 – 30 (or more!)
Age Range: elementary school – adult
Intensity: Mental: easy................♦.........hard
Physical: easy..♦.......................hard
Time: 5 – 10 minutes (without debrief)
Space: minimal...♦......................lots
Set Up Time: 1 minute
Amount of Duct Tape Required: approximately 12 feet for each set of Consensus Loops
View Video: www.DuctTapeTeambuildingGames.com
Username: duct Password: tape

Game Objective

Determine which of the duct tape loops is holding the other four loops together.

Skills Developed

Problem Solving, Conflict Management

Set Up / Preparation

Create a set of "Consensus Loops": Start with a strip of duct tape approximately 30 inches long and then fold it in half lengthwise (sticky sides together). Now pull off a short strip of duct tape and use it to connect the ends of this strip together to make a loop. Repeat this process to make a total of 5 loops. NOTE: Use the fifth duct tape loop to connect the previous four loops together (like a key ring). You'll need one set of Consensus Loops for each small team (2 - 5 people).

Presenting the Challenge

1. Prior to starting the game, show the group one of your Consensus Loops sets. Hold up the one loop that acts like a key-ring to the other four loops.
2. Create groups of about 2 - 5 people. Supply each group with their own Consensus Loops set. When you do this, place the loops on a table or on the ground next to the group in such a way that the group can start the activity without touching the

loops. Depending on how you put the Consensus Loops on the ground, the activity will be easy or hard to complete. To make it easy, simply spread out the loops. To make it hard, crumple the loops into a ball.

3. Presentation Script: "Your challenge is to work collaboratively to identify the one loop that acts like the key-ring to the other four loops." [read the rules below]

Rules

1. The loops may not be touched or moved during the decision making process.
2. The group must reach consensus as to which loop acts like the key-ring to the other four loops prior to touching the loop to determine if their choice is correct.

Safety Warning

Do not operate heavy machinery while playing the Consensus Loops game because staring at the Consensus Loops too long can result in a meditative state which can lead to a deep sound sleep and this is not conducive to operating heavy machinery.

Story Line

"While visiting the planet Ductapicus, you've encountered a strange snake that you want to keep as a live specimen to share with the science community on Earth. The snake is highly venomous and so you must be careful when picking it up. If you grab it by the loop in its body that connects the other loops the snake is completely docile."

Facilitator Notes

I use this activity to begin discussions about group problem solving strategies and how we can go about reaching consensus.

Achieving true consensus is difficult. It requires serious treatment of every group member's considered opinion.

To learn more about how to use consensus in teams I recommend accessing the resources at www.FacilitationFirst.com which is headed up by my good friend Michael Goldman.

Debriefing Suggestions

A neat way for a group to self-debrief this activity is to videotape the group as they go about solving this challenge and then play it back to them. Ask them what they observe.

What do we like about how we go about making decisions? What would we change?

When is reaching consensus useful for our team? When is it impractical?

Variations

1. To make the activity easier you can: have fewer loops (for example 3 loops in all rather than 5), or spread the loops out so that it's easier to see.
2. To make the activity harder you can bundle the loops tightly together before presenting them to the group, create Consensus Loops that have 7 or 8 loops per set or time the group ("You have 1 minute to correctly solve this challenge.")

History

I learned this activity from master team builder Jeff Long in the early 90's. This game was described in Jim Cain's award winning teambuilding games book entitled "Teamwork & Teamplay". **www.teamworkandteamplay.com**

Related Quote

"Whoever starts out toward the unknown must consent to venture alone" ~ **Andre Gide**

Crossover

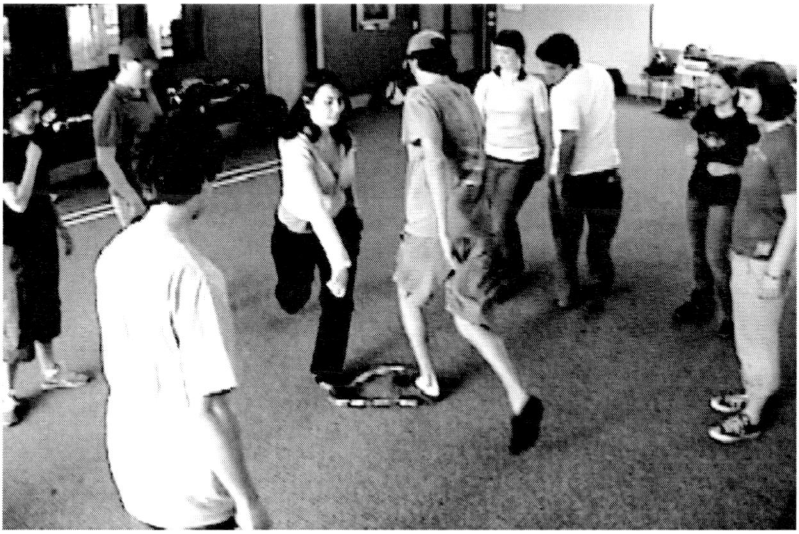

Group Size: 8 - 30

Age Range: middle school – adult

Intensity: Mental: easy...........♦..............hard

Physical: easy...........♦..............hard

Time: 10 - 20 minutes (without debrief)

Space: minimal...................♦......lots

Set Up Time: 1 minute

Amount of Duct Tape Required: approximately 5 to 6 feet

Additional Prop: One stopwatch

View Video: www.DuctTapeTeambuildingGames.com

Username: duct Password: tape

Game Objective

Team members must move from one side of a circle to the other as quickly as possible.

Skills Developed

Communication, Planning, Goal Setting, Creativity, Process Improvement

Set Up / Preparation

1. Create an open playing area free of obstacles.
2. Create a square or circle in the center of the playing area. To create a square, tear off four strips of duct tape, each measuring approximately 13 to 16 inches and then form a square on the ground. To create a circle, tear off one strip of duct tape measuring approximately 5 feet. You can then tape a circle to the ground or fold the tape in half lengthwise and then treat the duct tape like a piece of rope and simply lay this 5 feet long section of duct tape on the ground in the shape of a circle.

Presenting the Challenge

1. Ask the group to stand in a circle with the square at the center of the circle. Participants can't be touching anyone (includes hair and clothing).
2. Have the participants find a partner across the circle. Make sure everyone has only ONE partner. In case you have an odd number of people in the group you'll have one team of 3 - two will stand next to each other and the third member will be directly across the circle from them.
3. <u>Presentation Script:</u> "In a moment, but not now, I'm going to say "ON YOUR MARK GET SET GO!" and when I do, I'll start my stopwatch/timer and your job will be to trade places with your partner across the circle as fast as possible. Once everyone has traded places with their partner I'll stop the stopwatch. When you trade places with your partner you must travel through the center of the circle and touch the inside of the square/circle simultaneously." [read the rules below]

Rules

1. You may not rearrange yourselves in the circle. You must remain across the circle from your partner.

2. The square/circle may not be moved.
3. You may not touch anyone at any time during this activity (not even hair or clothing). The team will receive 10 seconds added to the score each time someone touches anyone else. The group must announce a touch when they see it. If the group fails to announce or identify a touch (i.e. attempting to hide or cover up a touch) then the penalty is doubled (20 seconds added to the final score).
4. When you trade places with your partner you and your partner must travel through the center of the circle and touch the inside of the square/circle simultaneously.

Safety Warning

1. Some people may want to run in this activity, which might be dangerous if they hit someone head on. If you suspect your group might create a head-on collision don't do this activity.
2. People with knee, ankle or back injuries should not participate.
3. Keep the playing area clear.
4. This game must be played on a flat surface.
5. Participants need to wear shoes appropriate for quick movement.

Story Line

"We've all come to acknowledge how important it is for people around the world to understand other people's points of view (position / situation). The faster we can understand the more fully we'll be able to help each other. This activity gives us an opportunity to (metaphorically) see the world from the perspective of someone opposite us (holding an opposing point of view). It also gives us the opportunity to practice a sense of urgency."

Facilitator Notes

1. After the group has completed their first attempt, announce the time from your stopwatch and then ask the team to beat that record. Allow the group multiple attempts in an effort to continually lower the score (time).
2. During an attempt, you (the facilitator) must watch for "touches" and then, for each touch, add 10 seconds to the final time. If the group doesn't identify a touch to the facilitator

(trying to hide it or cover it up) then a 20 second penalty is assessed for that touch. This rule makes it easier for you to run this activity.

3. A smaller group (10 people) will have a much easier time with this activity than a group of 30 or even 40. The larger groups typically have more difficulty with leadership and sharing ideas.

Debriefing Suggestions

A major theme of this activity is "continuous improvement". Therefore, consider focusing your discussion on the lessons learned and strategies practiced and how those same lessons and strategies can be applied in the "real world" (back at the office, etc.).

Variations

Experiment with the size of the square/circle in the center. The smaller the square/circle the harder the game gets. What if you made a square/circle with an inside area smaller than your hand?

History

This game was taught to me by master teambuilder Earl Davis of Moonshadow Learning Services **www.moonshadow.net**

Related Quote

"A mind not to be changed by place or time, the mind is its own place, and in itself can make a Heaven of Hell, a Hell of Heaven."
~ John Milton

Duct Tape Madness

Group Size: 9 – 30
Age Range: high school – adult
Intensity: Mental: easy............♦...........hard
Physical: easy..................♦......hard
Time: 5 – 10 minutes (without debrief)
Space: minimal..................♦......lots
Set Up Time: 5 minutes
Amount of Duct Tape Required: 20 - 30 feet
View Video: www.DuctTapeTeambuildingGames.com
Username: duct Password: tape

Game Objective

Get all the items from the center "container" into your own "container".

Skills Developed

Problem Solving, Competition / Cooperation

Set Up / Preparation

1. Create 50 small flat duct tape squares (pieces). To make one small flat duct tape square, pull off a 4 to 6 inch long strip of duct tape from the roll and then fold that strip in half (sticky sides together). Repeat this process to make 50 pieces.
2. Create four rings out of duct tape. These rings will measure approximately 7 to 8 feet in circumference. To make one ring, pull off a 7 to 8 feet long strip of duct tape and then fold the duct tape in half length wise - this makes one long strip of duct tape (7 to 8 feet long) with only the non-sticky side showing. To complete this ring, attach the ends together with a small piece of duct tape. Repeat this process to make the other rings (total of 4 rings).
3. Setup the playing area. The playing area needs to be large, flat and safe (free from anything that might trip someone up). This game can be played in a large indoor space or outside on a large flat surface (example: basketball court or soccer field). The larger the playing area the more energy the group will have to expend. Place one ring in the center of the playing area (called the "Center Ring") and place all 50 of the small duct tape squares (pieces) inside that ring. The other three rings (called "Team Rings") will be placed around the Center Ring. The Team Rings must be at an equal distance from the Center Ring. I recommend placing the Team Rings at least 25 feet away from the Center Ring.
4. Create a set of written directions for each of the three teams. When you present this game to the group (see below), you'll be dividing the large group into three smaller equal sized teams. As you'll see in the directions below, you'll be handing each team a set of written directions to start the game. It is possible to lead this game without preparing written directions in advance however I believe this game plays better if you provide written directions. Make three sets of written directions (one for each small team), each set saying the following:

OBJECTIVE: Get all the items from the center ring into your own ring. RULES: (1) Each person may carry only one item at a time. (2) Items must be carried (no throwing items). (3) Once the center ring is empty, you may take items from any other ring. (4) You may not guard any of the rings. (5) You win when all the items are in your ring. (6) Violation of a rule may result in a penalty.

Presenting the Challenge

1. Divide the large group into three smaller teams of equal size. It's not necessary that the teams are exactly the same size.
2. Ask each of the small teams to find and stand next to one of the three Team Rings (each small team will have their own Team Ring).
3. Provide each small team with a set of written directions. Do not allow the small teams to begin reading the written directions yet! The small teams will have to wait for your signal to begin reading the directions -the goal being to get all three small teams reading the directions simultaneously.
4. <u>Presentation Script:</u> "You'll notice that each of the three small teams has their own ring and there is a fourth ring in the center of the playing area filled with small pieces of duct tape. Each of the small teams also has a set of directions and when I say "READ YOUR DIRECTIONS" your team needs to quickly read your directions and when I yell "GO!" start playing the game making sure you follow all the written directions."
5. Allow the teams just enough time to read the directions and then shout, "GO!" The goal here is to force the teams to take action without planning. A frenzy of activity will ensue.

Rules

If you decide not to provide written directions to the small teams to read then you should read the following objective and rules aloud to the teams:

OBJECTIVE:

Get all the items from the center ring into your own ring.

RULES:

(1) Each person may carry only one item at a time.

(2) Items must be carried (no throwing or rolling of items).

(3) Once the central container is empty, you may take items from any other container.

(4) You may not guard any of the containers.

(5) You win when all the items are in your container.

(6) Violation of a rule may result in a penalty.

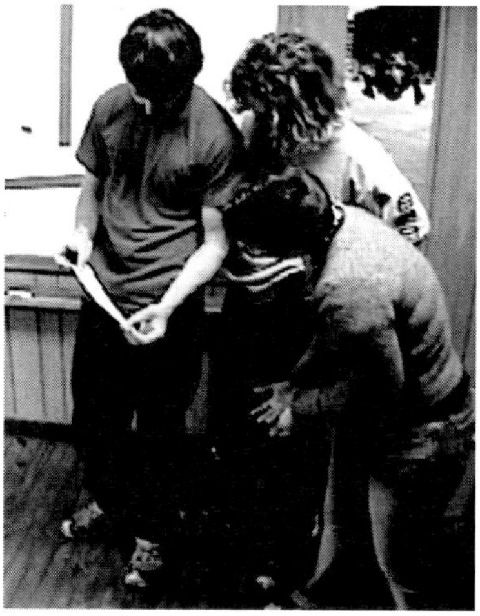

Safety Warning

Make sure the area you intend to run this activity in is free and clear of holes or things the participants could slip on.

Facilitator Notes

1. When you yell "GO!," the groups will have just enough information to begin taking action. If you wait too long and allow the groups to read through the information AND start to make a plan, they may decide to work cooperatively right off the bat (without going through all the frenzy).

2. When you yell "Go!" without allowing them to plan, they will usually run to the center ring and start grabbing pieces of duct tape. The Center Ring will quickly empty (within 60 – 90 seconds) and then the groups will begin taking pieces of duct tape from the neighboring rings. Usually within 3 or 4 minutes most will start to catch on that it's nearly impossible to win unless something changes. What needs to change? The way the group thinks. They must begin to think of a solution where everyone can win.
3. Most groups decide to cooperate by stacking ALL of the rings and then placing all of the pieces of duct tape inside the stack of rings. This is "legal" according to the rules.
4. This activity can work even better (i.e. people become more competitive) by getting the small work groups to do something competitive prior to this game. Any competitive activity will do. The point is to get them working in small teams and thinking competitively just before the Duct Tape Madness activity. By getting the small groups to play a competitive game prior to Duct Tape Madness I'm increasing the likelihood that everyone will work really hard during the Duct Tape Madness game which usually implies everyone learning the lessons at a deeper (more emotional) level.

Debriefing Suggestions

One way to debrief this game is to ask each of the small teams to sit together in discussion groups. I then ask these small groups to answer the following question:

Which type of thinking (consciousness) is most prevalent in our team (in society)?

- Lose – Lose
- Win – Lose
- Win – Win

I give the small groups 5 or 10 minutes to discuss and then we meet back as a large group to share insights.

Common insights include:

- Lose-Lose and Win-Lose require lots more energy than Win-Win.

- We must be on the lookout for Win-Win opportunities from the outset even when we've been "setup" to ignore them.
- One person can make all the difference in the world. NOTE – This will usually be an insight when one person is responsible for getting the group to stop the frenzy and come up with a Win-Win answer (i.e. stack the duct tape rings). All it takes is one committed person to see things differently AND have the courage and conviction to make their views known to the larger community.

True Story

I led this activity with the teaching staff of a public school. Just like every other group that plays this game, everyone ran around trying to win the game by placing all the pieces of duct tape in their own ring.

Then, as the group got tired of running, a teacher suggested letting one team win by placing all the duct tape pieces in their ring. The other two teams conceded defeat and everyone placed the duct tape pieces in the third team's ring.

During the debrief, we discussed win-lose (which is what they decided on), lose-lose, and win-win.

One of the teachers suggested that their solution (a win-lose solution) was more realistic. She argued that the "real world" doesn't play by win-win and they shouldn't teach that type of thinking to the kids. In the real world, she said, people are out to get you and you better watch out for yourself. No one in the room challenged this teacher. Even the principal was in agreement.

Imagine having these teachers work with YOUR child!

This team, by the way, was experiencing a number of very deep and difficult challenges.

Would you like to learn how to handle a situation like this? You can learn how in the "Teams In Trouble" 2-CD multimedia training program available at www.TeachMeTeamwork.com

Variations

To make the game more challenging, play loud music. This will make it more difficult for people to share ideas during the game.

History

I first learned this activity from Sam Skies who has authored many great books on team building activities including "Executive Marbles" and "Feeding the Zircon Gorilla". **www.doingworks.com**

Related Quote

"Truly great madness cannot be achieved without significant intelligence." ~ **Henrik Tikkanen**

The group FINALLY figures out how to create a win-win situation by stacking all of the team's duct tape rings.

Electric Hands

Group Size: 10 – 20
Age Range: elementary school – adult
Intensity: Mental: easy..♦.......................hard
Physical: easy..♦.......................hard
Time: 10 – 30 minutes (without debrief)
Space: minimal............♦.............lots
Set Up Time: 1 minute
Amount of Duct Tape Required: one roll of duct tape
View Video: www.DuctTapeTeambuildingGames.com
Username: duct Password: tape

Game Objective

Grab the roll of duct tape before the other team does.

Skills Developed

Communication, Fun, Energizer

Set Up / Preparation

This game requires one roll of duct tape and a coin.

Presenting the Challenge

1. Divide the group in half (Team A and Team B).
2. The two teams sit down and face each other - sitting shoulder to shoulder in two parallel lines (lines are approximately two to three feet from each other).
3. Team A holds hands and Team B holds hands.
4. The people at the end of the lines will be the "grabbers". They will be grabbing the roll of duct tape that is placed in between them.
5. You will sit at the front of the two lines (opposite the grabbers). Your job is to flip the coin so that the people sitting closest to you (the "instigators") can see if the coin landed on "heads" or "tails". If the coin is "heads", the instigators send a make-believe electric pulse down the line by squeezing the hand of their teammate sitting next to them. When the grabber at the end of the line feels the pulse (feels their hand being squeezed) they quickly grab the roll of duct tape - trying to grab it before the other team's grabber.
6. <u>Presentation Script:</u> "This is a competitive game. Your team (your side) is going to try and grab the roll of duct tape before the other side does. I will flip the coin at this end of the line and if it lands on "heads" then the two people closest to me will send a make believe pulse down the line by squeezing the hands of the persons next to them and they in turn will squeeze the hands of the persons next to them (and so on). If the person at the end of the line feels the pulse (hand squeeze) they should grab the roll of duct tape before the other side does." [read the rules below]

Rules

1. When the coin flipper flips the coin and the coin lands on heads, the instigators squeeze the hands of the persons next to them. By doing this, they are sending an imaginary "electric pulse" down the line to the grabbers - - each person squeezing the hand of the person next to him or her.
2. The grabbers must keep their grabbing hand on their knee until they feel the "electric pulse" (i.e. when they feel their hand being squeezed by the persons next to them).
3. The grabbers grab the roll of duct tape when they feel the "electric pulse".
4. The first grabber (the first team) to grab the roll of duct tape wins that round. You get one point when you win a round.
5. After each round, everyone on the team rotates - the grabber moves to the front of the line and becomes the instigator and everyone shifts down. This gives everyone a chance to be both an instigator and a grabber.
6. The Inadvertent Grab Rule: If the coin lands on TAILS, the instigators should NOT squeeze hands. If the instigator inadvertently sends a pulse down the line and the grabber grabs the roll of duct tape then that team loses a point.

Safety Warning

Do not allow participants to send actual electrical pulses through each others hands unless you have the system approved in advance by a qualified / certified electrician and even then you should have an ambulance crew on-hand because electricity is dangerous.

Story Line

"With one roll of duct tape left and two teams who want it, you've decided to have an Electric Hands showdown to determine once and for all (or at least for the next 10 minutes) who the owner of the roll will be."

Facilitator Notes

This activity is a competitive, we win – you lose game (pitting one team against another) but if you present it with care, the game will not become divisive. Present this game in a light; jovial atmosphere and people will likely have fun with it. Watch out for the people who are super aggressive (must win) and people who hate to lose because they may spoil the fun for everyone. Any game of this nature can get people worked up about winning and losing. Your job is to present it in such a way that fun is the most important outcome.

Debriefing Suggestions

I generally lead this activity for fun and I don't debrief it. However, this activity does present a great opportunity to discuss things like rumors and how they can travel with lightening speed (with positive and/or negative outcomes).

Variations

1. If you have an odd number of people, consider making one person the official coin flipper (a job normally reserved for the facilitator).
2. This activity works best with 7 to 10 people on each team. If you have more than 20 people, consider making multiple groups rather than making two really long lines.

History

I learned this activity from master team builder Betsy Hipple.

Related Quote

"One can never consent to creep when one feels an impulse to soar." ~ **Helen Keller**

Focus Ring

Group Size: 4 – 10
Age Range: elementary school – adult
Intensity: Mental: easy.........♦................hard
Physical: easy........♦.................hard
Time: 10 – 30 minutes (without debrief)
Space: minimal...................♦......lots
Set Up Time: 2 minutes (not including prop creation)
Amount of Duct Tape Required: 40 - 50 feet
View Video: www.DuctTapeTeambuildingGames.com
Username: duct Password: tape

Game Objective

Using the Focus Ring (made from duct tape!), carry a ball made of duct tape from one point to another.

Skills Developed

Communication, Problem Solving, Leadership

Set Up / Preparation

1. Create a Focus Ring out of duct tape (see detailed directions below).

   A. The Focus Ring is made up of two components: (1) Ropes, and (2) Ring.
   B. Making Ropes: Tear off approximately 6 feet of duct tape and then fold over on itself lengthwise (sticky sides together). This will make one long duct tape rope. When you tear of a length of duct tape that long it helps to stick one end to a desk and then slowly begin folding the sticky sides together (lengthwise) from the end not stuck to the table. One Focus Ring needs up to 10 sections of rope.
   C. Making a Ring: The finished Ring is 8 inches in diameter. Start by tearing off 12 inches of duct tape and then folding in half lengthwise (sticky sides together). Then fold in half lengthwise AGAIN. Now make a circle (ring) out of this 12 inch length of duct tape ensuring to overlap the ends by 4 inches -- this will produce an 8 inch diameter circle (ring). To hold this ring together (in this shape) use several short (2 to 3 inch) lengths of duct tape and tape it all in this shape.
   D. Attaching Ropes to Ring: Thread three inches of one end of one rope through the ring and then fold the rope around the ring loosely. Using a short (3 to 4 inch) section of duct tape, tape the end of the rope to itself. Don't tape the rope so tightly to the ring that it can't move - the duct tape rope should move easily around the ring. Continue adding ropes to the ring (each participant will need one rope).
2. Create a 4 to 5 inch diameter ball made of duct tape.
3. Create or find a playing area. You can get a sense of the playing area size through the photos.

Presenting the Challenge

1. Each person in the group holds on to the end of one of the duct tape "ropes" (one rope per person). The team then pulls back gently on the ropes and positions themselves equally around the center ring much like the spokes of a wheel.
2. Place (balance) the duct tape ball on top of the ring at the center of the Focus Ring.
3. <u>Presentation Script:</u> "Your challenge is to transport the duct tape ball while it's balanced on the ring from where you are now to a new location (show the group the new location)." [read the rules below]

Rules

1. Each participant operates their own duct tape rope.
2. Participants must hold onto the <u>end</u> of the duct tape rope and no other place.
3. Participants must remain at a distance of at least the length of a duct tape rope (very important).
4. If the duct tape ball falls off the ring the group must start again.
5. The Focus Ring device may not be altered.

Safety Warning

1. Do not allow participants to tie the duct tape rope around their hands or fingers.
2. When the group is moving (walking) along with the Focus Ring, all of their attention tends to be focused on the duct tape ball. This can cause a problem if the path the group is required to travel is dangerous in any way (they may not notice the danger!). As the facilitator of this activity you must make sure the path the group takes is safe and you must also warn the group of any hazards before and during the game.

Story Line

"While traveling through the Amazon jungle, your research team has come across a strange egg that appears to be from an alien life form. The egg is in danger of overheating so you must transport the egg to a safer and cooler area. You've noticed that anyone who gets too close to the egg starts to laugh uncontrollably so your team has built an alien egg transportation device out of duct tape. The egg is fragile, so be careful. Your team must act quickly because time is running out."

Facilitator Notes

1. This activity is quick and easy to lead. The time consuming part is making the Focus Ring and the duct tape ball.
2. If you have a Focus Ring already made and it has 10 duct tape "ropes" but if you only have only 6 participants you can either remove the extra ropes or allow some to operate two ropes.
3. This activity works best when there are between 4 and 10 participants. If you have more than 10 participants (16 for example) just make several sets of Focus Rings and divide the big group into smaller activity groups.

Debriefing Suggestions

1. One of the realities this game can teach well is the impact one person can have in a team. You can have a team of 8 where all but one is trying hard and that one person can make success impossible. If the group is dealing with a similar issue back in "real life" (office, home, etc.) this activity can act as a great opening to discuss this truth.
2. I often ask a group to identify their most important goal and then ask them to identify the biggest obstacles on the way to that goal. I then write the goal on the duct tape ball using a marker and then place physical objects (tables, chairs, doors, etc.) in the path of the group – I even identify each obstacle with an index card (example: table = lack of adequate time). Then I'll make the group travel under the table, over the chairs, through the door, etc. To debrief I'll ask the group to describe how they handled each of the physical obstacles and how they may be able to use similar skills to handle the real obstacles which apparently prevent them from achieving their goal.

Variations

1. Have the group transport the ball over, under or around chairs, trees, desks, doors, through a pool, etc.
2. Use a bigger ball (make one out of duct tape or use a basketball) to make this activity harder.
3. Using a black magic marker, write a number at the end of the duct tape rope. Then during the game, you can announce that only the person holding that particular number can talk. Allow him or her to talk for one minute and then change the number

allowing someone else to talk. This variation allows everyone to talk and take a leadership role.

4. Create a “pedestal” that the duct tape ball must be transported to and placed on top of, all without the ball falling off the pedestal. One way to create a quick pedestal is to turn a chair upside down and then on one leg of the chair, create a cylinder or cone out of duct tape. The cylinder or cone must be small enough in diameter for the ring in the Focus Ring to pass over the top of yet just big enough to balance the duct tape ball on top of. Refer to the photo. Have the group transport the ball from one location (outside the room) to the pedestal. The group is done when the duct tape ball is balanced on the pedestal and the group has released all of the duct tape ropes.

History

This game was taught to me by master teambuilder Jim Cain who coauthored the award winning book “Teamwork and Teamplay” **www.TeamworkAndTeamplay.com**

Related Quote

“The key to success is to focus our conscious mind on things we desire not things we fear.” **~ Brian Tracy**

Four Corner Traverse

Group Size: 16 – 24
Age Range: middle school – adult
Intensity: Mental: easy.................♦........hard
Physical: easy........♦.................hard
Time: 20 – 30 minutes (without debrief)
Space: minimal...........♦..............lots
Set Up Time: 5 minutes
Amount of Duct Tape Required: 40 - 50 feet
View Video: www.DuctTapeTeambuildingGames.com
Username: duct Password: tape

Game Objective

With four small teams located at the corners of a square, teams must switch places with the team diagonally opposite them.

Skills Developed

Trust, Communication, Leadership, Problem Solving, Creativity, Planning, Resource Management

Set Up / Preparation

1. Stepping Stone Cards: Create at least one "stepping stone card" for each participant. Stepping stone cards measure 4 x 5 inches (approximately) and are made out of duct tape (see photo below). Make at least 5 more stepping stone cards than you have participants. Consider having your participants make the cards with you as part of the activity.

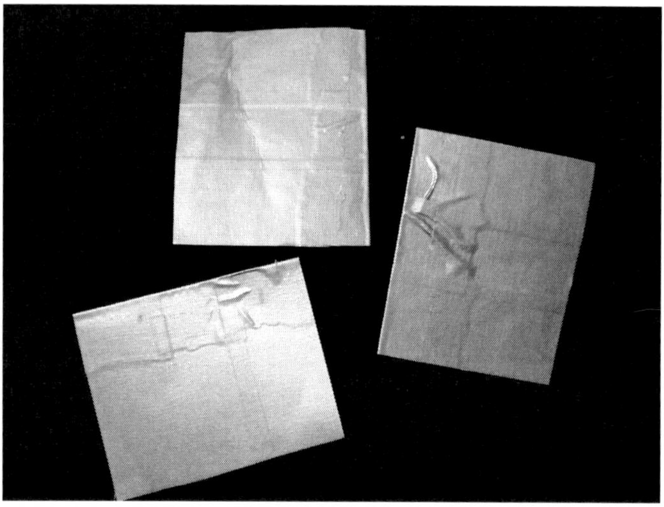

2. Playing Area: Create the playing area with a giant imaginary square in mind. Instead of actually taping a giant square on the ground you'll be marking the imaginary corners of this square with corner "tabs" (see the diagram below). The length of one side of this imaginary square is determined by the number of people in each of the small teams - if there are 5 people in each small team (at each corner), then the square is 5 normal paces long on each side. If there are 6 people in each small team then the square is 6 normal paces long on each side, and so on.

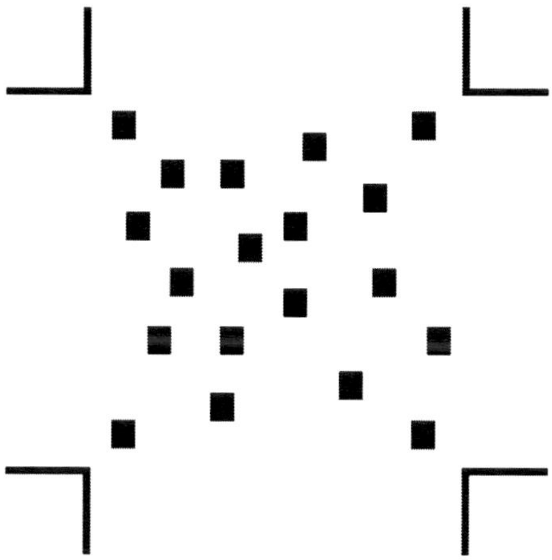

3. Stepping Stone Card Placement: Populate the area inside the imaginary square with the stepping stone cards (view the diagram above). The number of stepping stone cards is equal to the total number of participants. To make the game easier, place more cards in the playing area.

Presenting the Challenge

1. Divide the group into four smaller teams. Ask each team to pick and then stand behind one of the corner "tabs".
2. Presentation Script: "Your challenge is to travel from the space you're now in to the space diagonally across from you." [read the rules below]

Rules

1. When traveling from the space you're now in to your new space, you must use (step on) the duct tape stepping stone cards.
2. Your foot is allowed to touch the ground inside the playing area as long as part of your foot is touching a stepping stone card. NOTE: There is no limit to the number of people that can touch a stepping stone card at one time.

3. Before someone can exit the playing area, EVERYONE (from all 4 small teams) must be inside the playing area (touching a stepping stone card).
4. Once you exit the playing area you may not reenter.
5. Once a stepping stone card is touched (stepped on) someone must remain in physical contact with it at all times or that stepping stone card must be removed from the playing area and it will not be returned. If the facilitator detects that this rule is violated then the game starts over with everyone back in their original position.
6. Should someone step on anything other than a stepping stone card inside the playing area, that person must start over (walking back to their original starting position).
7. If anyone has two feet in the air at anytime (example: jumping) the game stops and everyone returns to their original corner and the game starts over.
8. Stepping stone cards may not be moved. EXCEPTION: The stepping stone card can rotate (spin like a CD) if needed.
9. If any person is unable to move to his/her final destination then the game starts over with everyone moving back to his/her original starting position.
10. The playing area and the stepping stone cards may not be altered.

Safety Warning

1. People with knee or balance problems should not play this game.
2. Stepping stone cards might slip out from under participants causing them to fall. Warn people about this possibility.

Story Line

"You're a group of gnomes living in a swamp and it's vacation time. Your family (team) has decided to travel to another area of the swamp and you must travel on top of the lily pads (stepping stone cards) because of hungry alligators in the water. Good luck!"

Facilitator Notes

1. To increase clarity, consider demonstrating some of the rules.
2. During the game, I typically walk slowly around the perimeter of the playing area looking for stepping stone cards that have been touched and then lost physical contact with. If the group loses contact with a card after touching it then watch to see if the group removes the stepping stone from the playing area (they should). If they don't, then call a stop to the game and announce what just happened and then start the game over (everyone back to their original spot).
3. It's normal for a group to make several attempts at this game before they experience success. The key to success is LOTS of communication.

Debriefing Suggestions

1. Teams that pay attention to their resources (stepping stones) tend to experience success. How did the group manage (care for) their resources? What did you like about how you managed your resources and what would you change? What resources are we currently managing well and what are the resources we mismanage?
2. Depending on the group and situation, you can use this activity as an opening to discuss people's beliefs about resources and supply. Consider reading the amazing book by the famous economist Paul Zane Pilzer entitled *Unlimited Wealth – The Theory and Practice of Economic Alchemy*. In his theory, Pilzer holds that we live in a world of unlimited economic resources. Gone is the concept of a "pie" (if you get a big slice than someone down the line must end up with a smaller one). This book will challenge you to look at resources in a new and exciting way.

Variations

1. To make the game harder, supply 2 or 3 fewer stepping stones than there are people.
2. To make the game easier, add more spots than there are people. You'll probably notice people "wasting" stepping stones (resources).

3. Provide a limited amount of time to complete the challenge.

History

I learned this game from master teambuilder and author Sam Sikes **www.doingworks.com**

Related Quote

"There is a space between man's imagination and man's attainment that may only be traversed by his longing." ~ **Kahlil Gibran**

Going All The Way

Group Size: 10 – 100

Age Range: elementary school – adult

Intensity: Mental: easy...♦.......................hard
Physical: easy..........♦...............hard

Time: 5 – 10 minutes (without debrief)

Space: minimal...................♦......lots

Set Up Time: 1 minute

Amount of Duct Tape Required: 10 - 20 feet

View Video: www.DuctTapeTeambuildingGames.com
Username: duct Password: tape

Game Objective

Working in teams of 5 people, move your piece of duct tape as far away from your team's start line as possible before time runs out.

Skills Developed

Problem Solving, Creativity, Goals, Resource Management, Leadership

Set Up / Preparation

1. Select an appropriate playing area for this game. An ideal space will be a long, empty, carpeted room. A flat, grassy, outdoor space can also work.
2. Create teams of 5 people.
3. Using a piece of duct tape, create a “start line” on the ground and have all teams stand behind the start line.
4. Supply each team with a six inch long piece of duct tape and ask them to fold it in half (sticky side together) to form a three inch piece of duct tape.

Presenting the Challenge

1. With all teams standing behind the start line and holding their piece of duct tape read the Presentation Script.
2. <u>Presentation Script:</u> “In this game, your small team is working independently of the other teams. You are in competition with the other teams. Your challenge is to move your piece of duct tape (or roll of duct tape) as far from the start line as you can. The team that moves their duct tape the farthest wins. The game starts when I say “On your mark, get set, go!” The game will be over in five minutes and I’ll let you know when you have only one minute left. You must follow all the rules.” [read the rules below]

Rules

1. When time is called, the team that has moved their piece of duct tape the farthest from the start line wins.
2. There must be a connection between the start line AND the piece of duct tape. Think of the connection between the start line and the piece of duct tape like a wire conducting electricity. There can be no breaks in that connection (a break

will disqualify you). It is permissible to extend or lengthen the connection using items on your person at the beginning of the game (example: shoe laces, belts, etc.).

3. The team may <u>not</u> use supplies <u>not</u> on their person when the game starts.
4. The start line may not be moved or altered. The piece of duct tape supplied to the team at the beginning of the game may not be altered (other than folding it in half).

Safety Warning

Some people can get carried away with this activity and really extend themselves physically. Watch out for people who may go too far and encourage them to be careful.

Story Line

"During ice fishing season accidents will sometimes occur causing a fisherman to fall through the ice. That's when the ice fisherman rescue crew is called in to help rescue the fisherman. Each year the ice fisherman rescue crews hold a competition to see which team can reach the farthest (reaching far is good in this business). The winning team at this year's competition wins a roll of duct tape! Good luck!"

Facilitator Notes

1. WARNING: Depending on your group, this game may result in participants who are partially clothed or even naked (i.e. they end up "going all the way"!). You might want to consider adding a fifth rule that addresses how much and what type of clothing people can remove to extend their reach from the start line to the piece of duct tape. I have seen very competitive groups quickly get down to their underwear. I've even seen a group tear up their t-shirts into long thin strips to extend their reach.
2. During the game I tend to walk among the teams so I can inspect the articles used to extend the line of connection from the start line to the piece of duct tape. If I see a break in the line I like to inform the team of the problem so they aren't surprised when I call time.

Debriefing Suggestions

1. This is a great activity to use as a lead in to discussions about commitment. How committed is the team to reaching its goal?
2. In this game the team that wins is usually very creative in how they use their resources (clothing) to extend their reach. This can give you the opportunity to discuss creativity. What resources are available to us now that we are underutilizing?
3. During play of the game you'll often see one team that is pushing the envelope and really playing full out. This usually causes the surrounding teams to play at a higher level. Who is our competitor? How can we help our competition? How can our competition help us?

Variations

1. This game works best if you have at least two groups competing with each other. If you have a small group (3 - 5 people) you can still play, just have the team work to set a "world record" on their own.
2. A very difficult variation is to require the groups to work with eyes closed (or blindfolds on). If you do this consider adding more time to the game (instead of 5 minutes give 10 minutes). Another option is to require the group to work for 1 minute with eyes closed - require this to happen in the middle of the game.

History

This game was created by master teambuilding gamesman Karl Rhonke **www.karlrohnke.com**

Related Quote

"There are two mistakes one can make along the road to truth...not going all the way, and not starting." ~ **Buddha**

Group Stride

Group Size: 10 – 60

Age Range: elementary school – adult

Intensity: Mental: easy....♦.....................hard

Physical: easy...........♦............hard

Time: 10 – 30 minutes (without debrief)

Space: minimal..................♦......lots

Set Up Time: 1 minute

Amount of Duct Tape Required: 10 - 20 feet

View Video: www.DuctTapeTeambuildingGames.com

Username: duct Password: tape

Game Objective

As a small team, advance (move) your strip of duct tape as far as you can from your start line.

Skills Developed

Goals, Process Improvement, Leadership

Set Up / Preparation

1. Select an appropriate playing area. The ideal playing area is a large, empty, carpeted room. A good alternative is a flat, grassy field.
2. This game requires a strip of duct tape for each small group. To make one strip pull approximately 12 inches of duct tape from the roll and then fold over lengthwise (sticky sides together). The end result is a 6 inch long strip of duct tape with no sticky sides showing. Alternatively, supply each group with a roll of duct tape (no need to pull tape off the roll).
3. Create a 12 inch long start line for each group.

Presenting the Challenge

1. Create teams of 4 or 5 people. It's nice (though not necessary) when all teams have an equal number of people.
2. <u>Presentation Script:</u> "Your challenge is to advance (move) your team's strip of duct tape as far as you can from the start line." [read the rules below]

Rules

1. Each team must create a "batting order" so that all team members take a turn in order.
2. Each team member gets one chance to advance the strip of duct tape. The first person starts behind the start line. To advance the strip of duct tape take one giant step and then reposition the duct tape at the tip of your foot furthest from the start line. The next person starts where the first person left off - standing behind the strip of duct tape and then taking one giant step to once again advance the strip of duct tape. This process continues until all team members have contributed to the advancement of the team's strip of duct tape.
3. Once all team members have had the opportunity to contribute to the advancement of the strip of duct tape the team is finished. The team must now place a piece of duct tape on the

ground to mark how far they've been able to advance the strip of duct tape (i.e. mark their record).

Safety Warning

1. Participants with back or knee problems should not participate in this game.
2. Some participants may overextend themselves when advancing the strip of duct tape which may result in injury. Warn participants about the potential for injury if they overextend themselves and caution them against it.

Story Line

"While on a mission to explore an icy moon of Jupiter, your team's space ship breaks down. To complete the repair your team must move a special piece of repair tape (it looks like duct tape) to the back of the ship (outside the ship). The outside temperature is so cold that you can't stay outside the ship for long. Each team member has just enough time to travel outside the space ship and move the repair tape one giant step towards the needed repair spot before needing to returning to the inside of the ship. You have just enough oxygen for all team members to have one attempt each. Good luck!"

Facilitator Notes

1. When I lead this activity I always give the teams a second attempt so they can try to beat their initial record. 99% of the time teams will beat their initial record and this provides a great opening for the debrief (see below). IMPORTANT - Do not tell the group at the beginning that you plan to give them a second attempt; otherwise the game will not play as well. Announce the second attempt AFTER the first attempt is over.
2. I recommend against setting this game up as a competitive event (i.e. small teams competing). I do admit it is tempting to have small teams compete against each other to move the strip of duct tape (or roll of duct tape) the farthest. Having the small teams compete, however, takes away from the primary message I like the teams to explore (see "Debrief Suggestions" below).

3. I like to have teams with at least 5 members each although it still works with teams as small as 4 people. I find teams larger than 8 people are too big because team members are not as engaged as in smaller teams.

Debriefing Suggestions

This activity creates a great opening to discuss goals. After the group completes the second round and exceeds their goal of advancing the strip of duct tape farther than the first attempt, ask the small teams to discuss why this happened. Questions you might ask include:

- What role do goals play in your life / on this team?
- What makes an effective goal?
- What makes an ineffective goal?
- Why are "stretch goals" (goals that make you stretch) important?

Variations

1. Instead of giving the group only two rounds (attempts) to move the strip of duct tape, give them three. Be aware that it's more likely for groups not to surpass their second round mark (goal).
2. Pair up teams at the beginning of the game. Team A starts on one side of the room and Team B starts on the other side of the room. The goal is for the two teams to meet in the middle of the room. The debrief can center around the effort and skills required to "reach out" to another team (or person).

History

I was taught this game by master teambuilder Jeff Long.

Related Quote

"When you engage in systematic, purposeful action, using and stretching your abilities to the maximum, you cannot help but feel positive and confident abut yourself." ~ **Brian Tracy**

Guard the Roll

Group Size: 8 – 20
Age Range: elementary school – adult
Intensity: <u>Mental</u>: easy....♦.....................hard
<u>Physical</u>: easy..................♦......hard
Time: 5 – 10 minutes (without debrief)
Space: minimal..................♦......lots
Set Up Time: 1 minute
Amount of Duct Tape Required: one roll
View Video: www.DuctTapeTeambuildingGames.com
Username: duct   Password: tape

Game Objective

Retrieve (rescue) the roll of duct tape from the center of the circle without getting tagged by the person guarding the roll of duct tape.

Skills Developed

Fun, Energizer

Set Up / Preparation

This game requires one roll of duct tape (you won't be pulling any tape off the roll though).

Presenting the Challenge

1. This game requires a lot of room to play. A large empty room or a flat grassy field work best.
2. Gather the group in a circle. Place the roll of duct tape in the center of the circle.
3. Ask for a volunteer - this person will be assigned the responsibility of guarding the roll of duct tape. The guard is to stand in the center of the circle near the duct tape to start the game. The rest of the group stands at a distance of approximately 20 feet from the center.
4. Presentation Script: "The challenge is for the person in the center of the circle to both guard the duct tape (keep it from getting grabbed) AND tag as many people as possible. Everyone else is trying to grab (rescue) the duct tape without getting tagged. If someone gets tagged by the Guard, he or she is out of the game and must wait until the next round to play again." [read the rules below]

Rules

1. The Duct Tape Guard may not step on, lie on top of or otherwise take the roll of duct tape out of play.
2. Anyone tagged by the Guard is out of the game until the roll of duct tape is grabbed (rescued) and a new round starts.
3. The roll of duct tape is rescued when someone grabs it AND gets away without being tagged. You only have to escape to a point at least 10 feet from where the roll of duct tape was originally placed on the ground at the center of the circle.
4. If someone grabs the duct tape and gets tagged before he can get far enough away from the center of the circle then the duct

tape is placed back at the center of the circle and play starts again (the tagged person is not allowed to play again until the next round).

5. No throwing or handing off the duct tape.
6. The person who rescued the roll of duct tape is now the Duct Tape Guard for the next round or that person the can choose someone to be the new Guard.

Safety Warning

1. People with knee or ankle problems should not play this game.
2. Play in a big safe area. The play area must be flat and free from any hazards that might harm the participants.

Story Line

"A troubled and misguided troll has stolen your community's only roll of duct tape and you must get it back. Don't let the troll tag you or you'll turn to stone!"

Facilitator Notes

1. Occasionally you'll find someone who is exceptional at guarding the roll of duct tape. No one will be able to grab the roll of duct tape and nearly everyone will end up getting tagged. If this happens you might need to give the group a 30 second count down to end the game and start the next round (with a new duct tape guard).
2. I've used this game as a segue way into a discussion about how there are some ideas, beliefs, or habits that we closely guard or are protective of. Sometimes these ideas, beliefs, or habits are beneficial to us and sometimes not. When they aren't beneficial it may take a community (group of friends, family, etc.) to "dislodge" or remove a negative influence - just like in this game. What are our responsibilities to each other when we notice a negative influence? When do we (the community) take action to help one of our own "wake up" to this negative influence?

Debriefing Suggestions

Questions to pose to the group:

What are you protective of in your life right now? (time, money, relationship, etc.)

What are you protective of that you need to let go of?

In this game you had to risk something to get the roll of duct tape. What are you currently pursuing in your life that is worth taking a risk?

Variations

1. Have two people protecting the roll of duct tape.
2. Provide a time limit to play the game (example 2 minutes) and then switch Guards.
3. Have multiple rolls of duct tape that need to be guarded by multiple people. Place the rolls close together and then spread them farther and farther away from each other. Notice how the strategy changes for both the guards and the people trying to grab the duct tape. Explore the lessons of this with the group.

History

This game was taught to me by master teambuilder Elbert Hargrave.

Related Quote

"Let not a man guard his dignity, but let his dignity guard him."
~Ralph Waldo Emerson

Hacky Bird

Group Size: 6 - 15
Age Range: elementary school – adult
Intensity: Mental: easy.....♦....................hard
Physical: easy........♦.................hard
Time: 5- 10 minutes (without debrief)
Space: minimal............♦.............lots
Set Up Time: 1 minute (not including prop creation)
Amount of Duct Tape Required: 10 - 20 feet
View Video: www.DuctTapeTeambuildingGames.com
Username: duct Password: tape

Game Objective

Keep the Hacky Bird in the air by hitting it 21 times.

Skills Developed

Communication, Planning, Goal Setting

Set Up / Preparation

Build a Hacky Bird out of duct tape.

1. The Hacky Bird is made up of two components: (1) Ball, and (2) Feathers.
2. Making the Ball: The aim is to make a ball the size of a tennis ball. Start by loosely crumpling up wads of duct tape. Once you have a large enough wad, make the ball covering by loosely wrapping the outside of the wad with duct tape. If you were to squeeze the ball you could easily crush it. Do not make a ball with a tight, dense center because it will hurt people's hands when they hit it.
3. Making the Feathers: To make one duct tape feather, pull off two 8-inch long strips of duct tape and then, with the two sticky sides facing each other, stick the two sections of duct tape together (creating one piece that is 8 inches long). You'll need to create 4 duct tape "feathers" for each Hacky Bird ball.
4. Attaching Feathers to the Ball: The job of the feathers is to slow down the flight of the ball while making it easier for participants to track (watch) through the air (this makes it easier to hit). To attach the feathers to the ball, fold each feather in half lengthwise and while holding the end of a feather at the "equator" of the ball, tape the feather to the ball. Space the feathers out equally as you tape them on. Folding the feather in half lengthwise before you tape them on helps give the feathers shape, enough shape to help the feathers do their job. Finally, tape all the feathers together just above the ball using a 6-inch strip of duct tape that is half the normal width (see photos). This final step will make the fall shape stand out while clumping the feathers together which makes the feathers work better.

Presenting the Challenge

1. Gather the group in a circle and allow everyone a chance to hit the Hacky Bird with their hand a couple of times just to get the feel of what it's like. After everyone's practiced hitting the Hacky Bird present the following challenge (read the Presentation Script).

2. <u>Presentation Script:</u> "Your challenge is to keep the Hacky Bird in the air by hitting it 21 times in a row." [read the rules below]

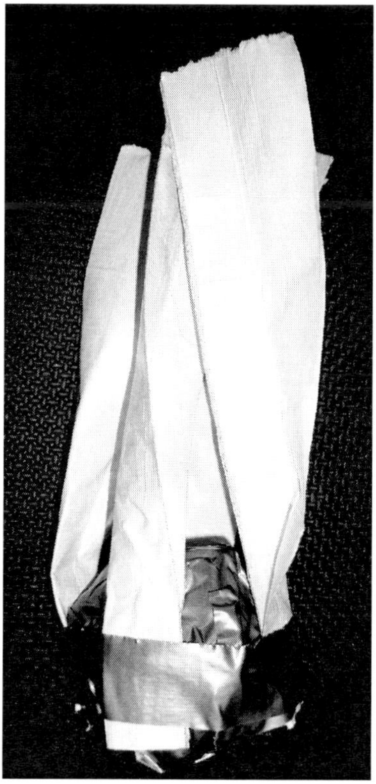

Rules

1. If the Hacky Bird hits the ground the group must start over.
2. The same person may not hit the Hacky Bird twice in a row. If this happens the group must start over. The same person can hit it more than once, but not twice in a row.
3. It's OK to hit the Hacky Bird with your foot to keep it in the air.

Safety Warning

1. Make sure the playing area is safe and clear of obstacles that could injure the participants.

2. Do not allow diving to hit the Hacky Bird. Diving to hit the Hacky Bird could result in injury.
3. Require participants to hit the Hacky Bird in an upward direction. Hitting the Hacky Bird straight ahead could cause injury if the Hacky Bird hits someone in the face.

Story Line

"You are a team of archeologists and you've encountered a mysterious and ancient temple. There is a secret door to the temple that will only open if you're able to hit a magical stone (Hacky Bird) in the air 21 times in a row."

Facilitator Notes

1. It's easiest to hit the Hacky Bird underhand (like in volleyball).
2. Hacky Birds are like a hand version of "Hacky Sack".
3. I like using the Hacky Bird at the beginning of a program to energize people and have some fun. It's a great portable activity that focuses the energy of the group.

Debriefing Suggestions

I typically have a group participate in Hacky Bird activities to have fun and focus the energy of the group. If I debrief it at all I generally ask this question: What did you like about how the group played this game that you would like to see continue throughout the program? The idea behind this question is to get a couple of quick sharing of views and then move on with the positive energy and focus.

Variations

1. Keep the Hacky Bird in the air for as long as possible (go for a record).
2. Hit it 21 times just like the original challenge and add the following – you must say your name when you hit the Hacky Bird. This is a great variation to do at the beginning of a program when people might not know each other's names.
3. Hit it 21 times just like the original challenge and add the following – when you hit it, you must say someone's name in the group AND you can't say the same person's name twice.

NOTE: The person whose name you say does not have to hit it after you.

4. Hit it 21 times just like the original challenge and add the following – spin around 360 degrees before you can hit it again.
5. Use your non-dominant hand to hit the Hacky Bird.
6. Ask the group to keep TWO Hacky Birds going simultaneously (it's very hard).

History

This game was taught to me by Jim Cain who coauthored "Teamwork & Teamplay **www.TeamworkAndTeamplay.com**

Related Quote

"Intelligence without ambition is a bird without wings."

~ Salvador Dalí

Helium Roll

Group Size: 8 – 12

Age Range: middle school – adult

Intensity: Mental: easy...................♦......hard

Physical: easy........♦.................hard

Time: 20 – 60 minutes (without debrief)

Space: minimal.........♦................lots

Set Up Time: 5 minutes

Amount of Duct Tape Required: One roll of duct tape (no need to pull tape off)

View Video: www.DuctTapeTeambuildingGames.com

Username: duct   Password: tape

Game Objective

Lower the roll of duct tape to the ground.

Skills Developed

Problem Solving, Communication, Goals

Set Up / Preparation

It's easy to prepare for this game - all you need is a roll of duct tape (you won't be pulling tape off for this game). The newer the roll of duct tape (the heavier the roll) the quicker and easier it is for the team to complete this game. Lighter rolls of duct tape (rolls that are almost used up) make it much more difficult for the group to experience success quickly.

Presenting the Challenge

1. Circle up the team in a tight formation.
2. Everyone extends their right arm and holds out their index finger at chest level (like they are pointing at someone). From above it will look like the spokes of a wheel.
3. You (the facilitator) then announce that you'll be placing a roll of duct tape on top of their index fingers. THIS PART IS IMPORTANT - when you place the roll of duct tape on their fingers, KEEP YOUR HAND ON TOP OF THE ROLL OF DUCT TAPE to prevent the group from raising it in the air. Apply just enough pressure on top of the roll of duct tape to prevent the group from lifting it up. It seems every group I've worked with wants to raise the roll of duct with their fingers even before they understand or know the directions (it's kind of weird actually!).
4. <u>Presentation Script:</u> "Your directions are as follows: As a group, you must lower this roll of duct tape to the ground without even a single person on the team losing contact with the roll. Should someone lose contact with the roll you must start again." [read the rules below]
5. After reading the above directions (script), release your hand from the roll of duct tape and step back.

Rules

1. No one may lose contact with the roll of duct tape. If anyone loses contact with the roll the entire group must start again. The starting position is the same as described above.

2. Only the index finger on the right hand can be used. The index finger must be placed below (underneath) the roll of duct tape. Nothing else is allowed to touch the roll. The roll may not be altered from the way it was originally presented.
3. Index fingers much remain rigid and straight (like you're pointing at someone).
4. Fingers and hands may not make contact with anyone else during the game.

Safety Warning

Depending on the group, this activity may not be appropriate due to the close proximity with which the team must work together.

Story Line

"You are a team of scientists and you've recently discovered a new energy source (a machine) that uses a roll of duct tape as a crucial component. The problem is the roll of duct tape must be lowered into the machine by all team members in a very specific way; otherwise the machine won't work. Good luck! I know your team can do it!"

Facilitator Notes

1. This is a very challenging game to complete without cheating (without losing contact with the roll of duct tape). If a group is fully honest about losing touch, then it could take as long as 60 minutes to complete. Because of this, do not do this game if the team is experiencing serious conflict.
2. Here's what typically happens in this activity: When you (the facilitator) give the directions and then release the roll of duct tape, the group will most often RAISE the roll (not lower it)! The group will usually laugh and find this somewhat strange. It is likely to take several attempts to just keep the roll steady (not lowering or raising).
3. This is a communication intensive activity where each person must be absolutely committed to doing his or her part. People will usually get frustrated and it's common to see some blaming occur.

4. The group will probably throw out many ideas on how to solve this challenge. What is usually observed is the entire group focusing, doing his/her job with the direction of one leader. Groups that have the most difficulty are usually all talking at once.
5. You may have to stop this activity several times mid-stream to help the group process how they are approaching this activity.
6. Why is this game called “Helium Roll”? When you first place the roll of duct tape on the participants’ fingers and then release it the group inevitably *raise* the roll. It’s as if the roll is made of helium and wants to float away.

Debriefing Suggestions

I’ve successfully used this activity to help the leadership of an organization create valuable distinctions between having a vision and realizing that vision. I did this by leading the group in a four-hour company vision statement workshop. After everyone was in agreement about the vision statement I had the group do the Helium Roll activity. Here is the metaphor I shared with the group: the roll was the company vision and by successfully lowering it to the ground they achieved their vision. What happened next was eye opening! The roll immediately went in the OPPOSITE direction from where they were trying to go – UP! After 50 minutes of trying to lower the roll to the ground they succeeded. “What were your key learnings?” I asked. Their response: everyone must be committed to the vision AND the process. Blaming and excuses won’t help you realize the vision any quicker. Staying calm and focused is critical to success especially when you think it can’t be done.

Variations

1. Have people pair up and supply each pair with one roll of duct tape. Have each pair lower their own roll to the ground so they can experience success. Then have people form groups of 4 and then provide them with a roll to lower. Continue making bigger groups until you have everyone working together on roll.

2. Start by giving the group a new (heavy) roll of duct tape. After the group accomplishes this, give them a nearly used up (lighter) roll of duct tape.
3. Require the group to complete this challenge with no verbal communication.

History

This activity was taught to me in the early 90's by master teambuilder Viva Pizer.

Related Quote

"Float like a butterfly, sting like a bee." ~ **Muhammad Ali**

Hidden Numbers

Group Size: 5 – 40

Age Range: elementary school – adult

Intensity: Mental: easy..................♦.......hard

Physical: easy...♦......................hard

Time: 5 – 10 minutes (without debrief)

Space: minimal.....♦....................lots

Set Up Time: 1 minute

Amount of Duct Tape Required: 8 feet

View Video: www.DuctTapeTeambuildingGames.com

Username: duct Password: tape

Game Objective

Participants must solve the puzzle by discovering the hidden numbers.

Skills Developed

Problem Solving, Creativity

Set Up / Preparation

1. This game requires 4 strips of duct tape. To make one strip pull approximately 24 inches of duct tape from the roll and then fold over lengthwise (sticky sides together). The end result is a 12 inch long strip of duct tape with no sticky sides showing.
2. Arrange the 4 strips of duct tape in columns on the floor.

Presenting the Challenge

1. Gather the group in front of you so that everyone can view the 4 strips of duct tape.
2. Presentation Script: "I'm going to show you a number between zero and ten. Your challenge is to correctly determine which number I'm showing you."
3. Reposition one strip of duct tape so it is perpendicular to the other three. You should use some theatrics here by acting like you are trying to make a particular shape (in reality the shape makes no difference to what you're really doing, but the group begins to think it does).
4. After you've rearranged the duct tape strips on the ground, slyly place your hands on your thighs and ask "What number is this?" The group will look at the shape you've created with the duct tape strips and make a guess. Ask for a couple of answers, then tell them the answer.
5. HERE'S THE TRICK: You must show the "number" with your fingers, which are on your thighs. If the number is 10, then you keep 10 fingers out. If the number is zero then you keep two fists on your thighs. If the number is 7, then you would have five fingers on one hand and 2 on the other hand with the "extra" fingers folded under.
6. After the first guess by the group, make another design with the duct tape strips on the floor. You can even act like you are making a pattern if you want. This only serves to distract people further. When the rearranging is done, place your hands on your thighs again and ask "What number is this?" If

the group is slow to pick up on it, confirm that the "number is right in front of you."

7. If the group has a very difficult time solving this puzzle, tell them you will make it more obvious as to what the number is. After fiddling around with the duct tape strips, REALLY emphasize putting your fingers on your thighs (being somewhat theatrical). You may even wiggle your fingers so people will notice them. If they still don't get it, take the duct tape strips away and ask the group "What number is this?" while emphasizing your fingers.

Rules

There are no real rules for this game. It's all in the presentation (see above).

Safety Warning

Do not play this game if wild animals (elephants, zebras, jackals, etc.) are loose in the room. Wild animals are unpredictable and dangerous.

Story Line

"Your team is traveling through a mystical land in search of answers to life's greatest questions. Your team comes to a bridge you must cross and to gain access to the key locking the bridge's gate, you must solve the puzzle of the Hidden Numbers. Good luck!"

Facilitator Notes

It's possible that someone in your group knows the answer to this activity before you even start (i.e. someone has played it before). If you suspect this, consider making an announcement that goes something like "If you are familiar with the activity I'm about to lead, please keep your responses to yourself and covertly observe your teammates."

Debriefing Suggestions

Oftentimes in life the solution to a problem is right in front of us but we don't see it because we allow ourselves to become distracted by extraneous information. In this case, the duct tape strips act as a distraction. People tend to focus so intently on the duct tape that they block out all other useful information. Some people will even argue that you were not showing the numbers with your fingers the entire time (when you really were). Potential questions to ask include:

- Are there any problems you're faced with right now that have an easy solution which you're not allowing yourself to see?
- What is it that distracts us as a team?
- What will cause us to gain clarity?
- What will change when we gain clarity?

Variations

1. I like to play this game while kneeling on the ground; however, you can lead this game sitting at a table (placing the duct tape strips on a table top).
2. I've led this game for a large group (100+) with a video camera projecting my image on to a large screen. In this situation I'll have people work in teams of 3 or 4 to solve the problem.

History

This game comes from master teambuilding gamesman Karl Rohnke **www.karlrohnke.com**

Related Quote

"Trust in dreams, for in them is hidden the gate to eternity."

~ Kahlil Gibran

The number is secretly revealed by the number of fingers you're showing.

Hole in Space

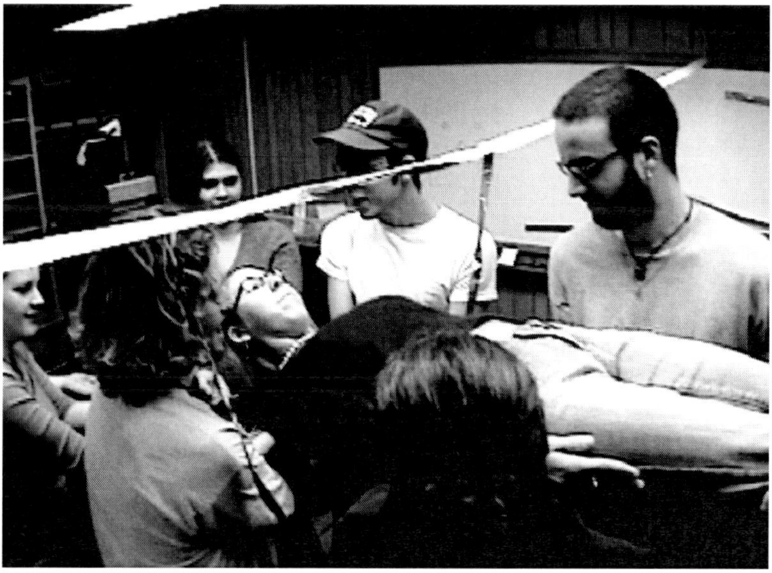

Group Size: 10 – 20
Age Range: high school – adult
Intensity: <u>Mental</u>: easy...................♦......hard
<u>Physical</u>: easy......................♦...hard
Time: 30 – 50 minutes (without debrief)
Space: minimal...................♦......lots
Set Up Time: 7 minutes
Amount of Duct Tape Required: 20 - 30 feet
View Video: www.DuctTapeTeambuildingGames.com
Username: duct Password: tape

Game Objective

Each group member must pass through a hole in space.

Skills Developed

Trust, Communication, Leadership, Roles & Responsibilities, Problem Solving, Planning, Resource Management

Set Up / Preparation

1. Decide on a safe location to lead this activity. An ideal location has a floor that is cushioned / padded - this helps reduce the likelihood of injury should someone fall during the game. The ideal location is also flat and easy to walk on.
2. Create the "Hole in Space" by first running a long piece of duct tape from one wall to another (approximately 5 or 6 feet off the ground). Next create the "hole" out of a strip of duct tape measuring 5 to 6 feet long (the shorter the piece of duct tape used to make the hole the harder the challenge). This short strip of duct tape should be attached to the long piece of duct tape (spanning the room) in two places so it creates a big hole or opening as it hangs (refer to photos).

Presenting the Challenge

1. Teach the group how to safely lift and spot team members. Use the safety guidelines at the beginning of this book to help you.
2. Divide the group in half, sending one half to one side of the Hole in Space and the other half to the other side of the Hole in Space.
3. Presentation Script: "Your challenge is to get your entire small team through the Hole in Space (travel through the Hole in Space) to the other side. Your two small teams are to work collaboratively. " [read the rules below]

Rules

1. No one may touch the duct tape. If someone touches the duct tape, a penalty will be applied. [examples: one person must go back, one side must stop talking for 3 minutes]
2. The flow of team members through the Hole in Space must alternate equally. When Side A sends a team member through

the hole, the next person through the hole must be from Side B. This pattern must continue.

3. No other equipment or tools may be used to help in the process (no tables, chairs, etc.).
4. No one can break the plane under the long string of duct tape (other than traveling through the hole). If the plane is broken a penalty will be applied.
5. No unsafe behavior. Jumping through the hole is forbidden. Launching people through the hole is forbidden.

Safety Warning

1. It's important to teach proper spotting techniques prior to giving the group this challenge.
2. Do not allow participants to hit their head or spine on the ground. This is very important. As the facilitator, you must be ready to jump in should you see a problem with the way the group is lifting or spotting team members.
3. If your group is not strong enough (physically), mature enough and/or calm enough, do not attempt this activity.

Story Line

"Your team has arrived at the International Space Station (ISS) and must enter through a small porthole. Due to an unstable situation caused by docking the Space Shuttle with the Space Station, your team must enter the Space Station one at a time and for each person that enters, one person on the Space Station must exit."

Facilitator Notes

A high degree of trust is required to successfully accomplish this challenge. This challenge is best left for a group that is fairly advanced as far as maturity and their ability to safely care for one another are concerned.

Debriefing Suggestions

Potential questions to pose to the group might be:

Who in your life lifts you up and helps you out during difficult and challenging times?

Which did you prefer, to lift people or be lifted? Why?

Variations

1. Experiment with the size of the hole. Smaller = Harder.
2. You can give the group an unlimited amount of time to complete this activity OR you can require the group to complete this activity in a limited amount of time (example: 25 minutes).
3. To make things more difficult, allow verbal communication only during an initial planning phase but not when the group carries out their plan.

History

This game was was originally described in one of Karl Rohnke's teambuilding games books. The "Hole in Space" was made from an automobile tire hanging between two trees.
www.karlrohnke.com

Related Quote

"Follow the rule of holes; if you are in one, stop digging."

~ Dennis Healy

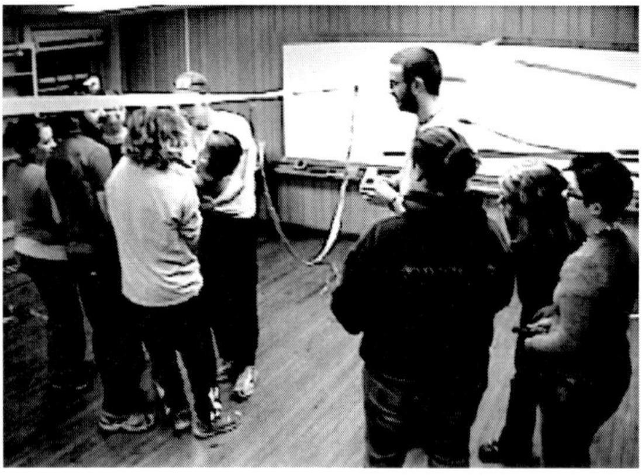

Human Knot

Group Size: 8 – 12
Age Range: middle school – adult
Intensity: Mental: easy.................♦........hard
Physical: easy...........♦..............hard
Time: 10 – 30 minutes (without debrief)
Space: minimal............♦............lots
Set Up Time: 5 minutes
Amount of Duct Tape Required: 16 - 20 inch piece for each person
View Video: www.DuctTapeTeambuildingGames.com
Username: duct Password: tape

Game Objective

The group must untangle itself to form a circle.

Skills Developed

Problem Solving, Communication, Planning

Set Up / Preparation

Create one "Tether" for each person. A Tether is made out of one strip of duct tape measuring 16 - 20 inches. After pulling a strip of duct tape off the roll, you must now fold it in half (sticky sides together) lengthwise.

Presenting the Challenge

1. Have everyone stand in a tight circle.
2. Each person places the Tether in their right hand and then extends their right hand (with the Tether) out across the circle to allow someone to grab their Tether with a left hand. If everyone has two hands, it doesn't matter if you have an odd or even number of people doing this activity - everyone will end up holding a Tether in both hands. You cannot allow two people to hold on to each other's Tethers (this will form a group of two and that's not good).
3. <u>Presentation Script:</u> "Now that everyone is holding a Tether you are essentially all tangled up. Your challenge is to untangle yourselves." [read the rules below]

Rules

1. You may never let go of the Tethers.
2. During the initial setup, you can't hold someone's Tether next to you.

Safety Warning

Those with an injury to their back, shoulder/arm, or neck are advised not to do this activity.

Story Line

"Due to miscommunication, your team has tangled itself into a big knot. You recognize that the ties that connect you (the Tethers) are valuable and letting go would signal defeat in the face of difficulty. Therefore, your goal is to untangle yourselves without letting go of your Tether!"

Facilitator Notes

1. This game can take as long as 30 minutes to complete.
2. The duct tape Tethers allow team members to twist and turn as they untangle themselves. The Tethers can also prevent the awkwardness of holding someone's sweaty hand for 5 or 15 minutes (or worse yet, having boys touch girls' hands – yuck!).
3. Due to the way the group initially created their knot (held each others' Tethers), the group may find they have created two or even three people circles. And it's not uncommon for the group to have some people facing in and some facing out in their people circle (this is OK).
4. If the group finds themselves all tangled up and unable to find a solution, offer the group the opportunity to have two people release and re-grip. If they still have difficulty, offer this re-gripping option again.

Debriefing Suggestions

What does it take to create/find a solution to a problem? This is the primary question I tend to ask a group after the Human Knot activity. The most common answer is "patience and perseverance".

Variations

1. Supply the group with a limited amount of time to complete the task (example: 20 minutes).
2. Require one person to start the game with his/her eyes closed. Then as the game progresses allow that person to see and then ask someone new to close his/her eyes. During the debrief, ask what it was like to play the game with their eyes closed. What lessons about teamwork did they learn?

History

Karl Rohnke first described this activity in his classic teambuilding games book "Silver Bullets". **www.karlrohnke.com**

Related Quote

"When you reach the end of your rope, tie a knot in it and hang on." ~ **Thomas Jefferson**

Infinite Loops

Group Size: people work in pairs
Age Range: middle school – adult
Intensity: Mental: easy............♦...........hard
Physical: easy.....♦....................hard
Time: 5 – 60 minutes (without debrief)
Space: minimal.....♦....................lots
Set Up Time: 1 minute
Amount of Duct Tape Required: 4 feet per person
View Video: www.DuctTapeTeambuildingGames.com
Username: duct Password: tape

Game Objective

Separate yourself from your partner.

Skills Developed

Fun, Communication, Problem Solving, Creativity.

Set Up / Preparation

Using four feet of duct tape, create one pair of Infinite Loops per person. Fold the four feet long strip of duct tape in half lengthwise (sticky sides together). Make the wrist loop by measuring 7 inches from both ends and fold the end of the duct tape strip at that 7 inch mark. Tape the end of the wrist loop using a separate piece of duct tape. When you're done, it should be easy to slip your hand into the wrist loops. Refer to the picture below.

Presenting the Challenge

1. Supply each person with one pair of Infinite Loops and have everyone insert their own hands into their own wrist loops.
2. Ask group members to pair up and then face their partner.
3. All partners are now to become connected. To connect, one person in the pair removes one hand from his wrist loop and then places the end of his Infinite Loop on the other side of his partner's and then reinserts his hand in his wrist loop. Refer to the photo below.

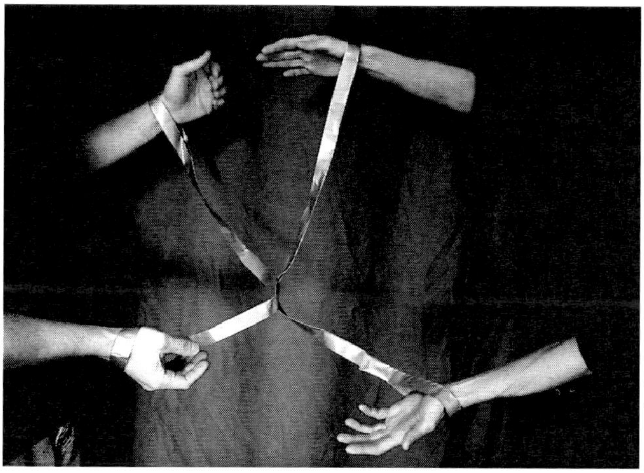

4. Read the Presentation Script.
5. Presentation Script: "Your challenge is to separate yourself from your partner (become disconnected)." [read the rules below]

Rules

1. Your wrist loops must stay on your wrists throughout the entire activity.
2. The Infinite Loops (duct tape) may not be cut, ripped, untapped, or otherwise altered in any manner.
3. If you become entangled during the activity you are permitted to take your wrist loops off and start over.

Safety Warning

Some people may get carried away during this game and, in an effort to find a solution, end up contorting their bodies which may be dangerous. If you see people getting into a potentially harmful position stop the game.

Story Line

"You've been captured by aliens from outer space who've attached a strange restraining device to your wrists. If you can find a way to disconnect from your partner you'll be able to escape. Good luck!"

Facilitator Notes

1. During this game I like to walk among the participants to observe how they are working out a solution. Be prepared to answer questions like "Are you sure there is a solution to this?"
2. This activity can take anywhere from a couple of minutes to an hour (or even longer) depending on how long it takes for people to solve the problem. When I was a high school teacher I would present this challenge and it might take a couple of days to solve because I would only allow students to work on it during the last 5 minutes of class.
3. You may want to offer people hints if the group is really struggling. I've found it's best to offer small hints first and only to the people who want hints.

The Solution

The following pictures demonstrate a solution.

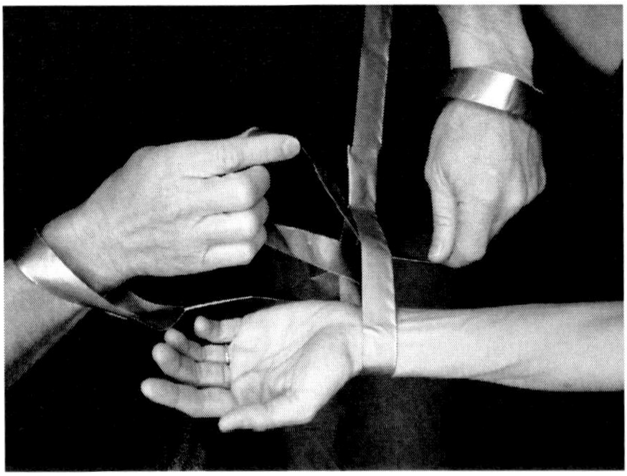

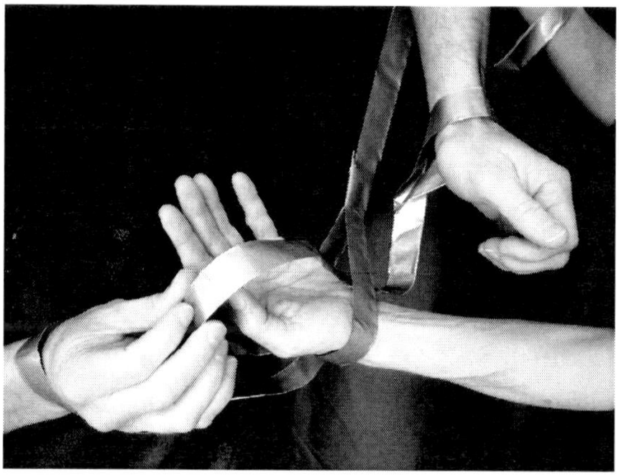

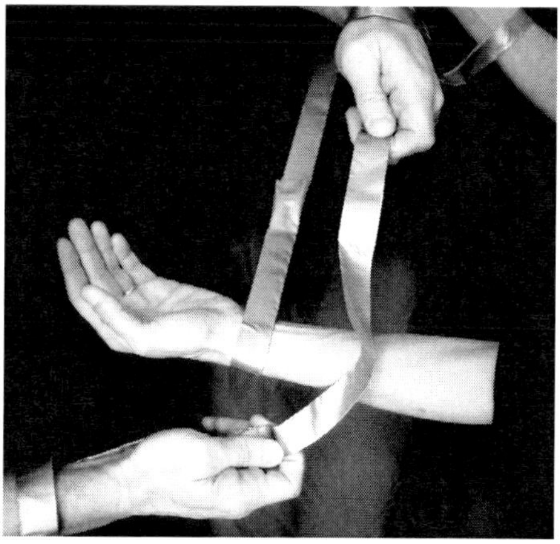

Debriefing Suggestions

I like to use this game to help people explore "dead ends" and the world of possibility because so many people who play this game can't see a solution to the problem.

Suggested questions include:

- At what point is it appropriate to give up when you can't find a solution?
- What can keep you going when a problem seems impossible to solve?

- Can you share a story of a time when you were faced with a seemingly unsolvable problem but you were able to find a solution?

Variations

1. If you have an odd number of people in the group you can create a group of three who work together to solve the problem. Have two people connect their Infinite Loops just like everyone else and then have the third person connect to either one of the people in the group of three. The same solution will be used.
2. Instead of placing the Infinite Loops on your writs, place them on your feet.
3. Supply each person with two sets of Infinite Loops - placing one set on their hands and the other set on their feet.
4. I've led this game with several hundred people with the following variation - I make an announcement at the beginning of the game in which I ask the first two people who solve this Infinite Loops puzzle to find me and then show me the solution. Once I'm convinced they can repeat the solution I ring a bell and ask everyone to stop. This is when I tell the large group that the game has changed. I announce that two people in the group know how to solve the problem - now the goal is to get everyone in the large group (all partners) to quickly learn the solution AND be able to demonstrate it when called upon. I let the group know I've started a timer and they must pick a representative to tell me when EVERYONE knows how to solve the problem. The goal here is for the group to practice teaching and learning quickly. Teams that are skillful at teaching and learning have a significant competitive edge in the marketplace.

History

This game comes from master teambuilding games leader Karl Rohnke. **www.karlrohnke.com**

Related Quote

""Finite to fail, but infinite to venture." ~ **Emily Dickinson**

Inhuman Knot

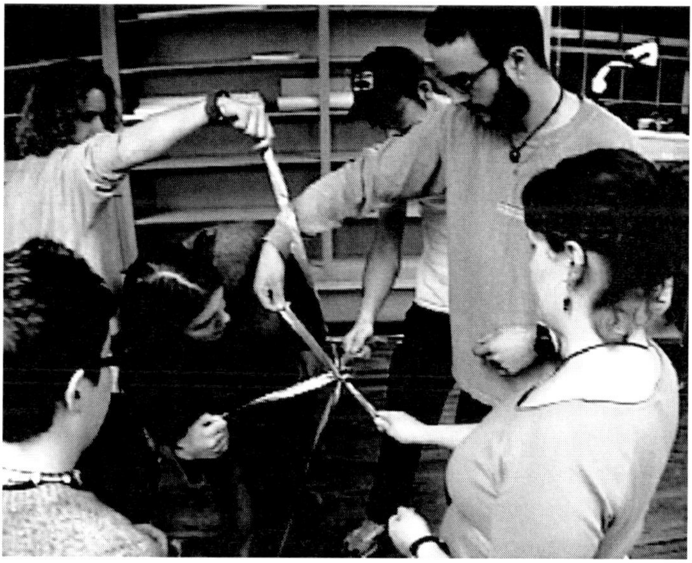

Group Size: minimum of 12 people (two groups of 6)
Age Range: middle school – adult
Intensity: Mental: easy............♦............hard
Physical: easy..........♦.............hard
Time: 10 – 20 minutes (without debrief)
Space: minimal..................♦......lots
Set Up Time: 5 minutes
Amount of Duct Tape Required: 32 - 36 inch piece for every two people
View Video: www.DuctTapeTeambuildingGames.com
Username: duct Password: tape

Game Objective

As a team, create a tangled mess of your tethers. Then trade your tangled mess with another group's and see if you can untangle their mess (while they untangle yours).

Skills Developed

Communication, Problem Solving

Set Up / Preparation

Create one "Tether" for every two people (a group of 6 people will need 3 Tethers). A Tether is made out of one strip of duct tape measuring 32 - 36 inches long. After pulling a strip of duct tape off the roll, you must now fold it in half (sticky sides together) lengthwise.

Presenting the Challenge

1. NOTE: This game requires at least 12 people (two groups of 6) to play.
2. You need one Tether for every two people.
3. People will be working in teams of 6. Setup the activity in advance by placing three Tethers on the ground in the shape of an asterisk (*). Each team of 6 will have their own set of Tethers in the shape of an asterisk.
4. Team members pick up an end of a Tether with one hand. Once you pickup a Tether you can't let go of it until the activity is over.
5. Each team of 6 will now take two minutes to tie a big knot in the center of the Tethers. Keep working on making the knot more tangled until time runs out. Remember, no letting go of the Tether!
6. When the time is up, lay your knotted Tethers (your tangled mess) on the ground and let go of the Tethers.
7. Teams will now rotate to another team's knotted Tethers and pick up the end of a Tether. Now work together to untangle the knot without letting go of the Tether.
8. <u>Presentation Script:</u> [*phase 1*] "Gather your team of 6 around a group of duct tape Tethers and position yourself next to the end of a Tether (one Tether end per person). Now, carefully pickup your Tether end with one hand while maintaining the star shape. When I say "go", your challenge is to create a tangled knot out of all Tethers in your team of 6 - when you're

doing this you may not let go of the end of your Tether! Ready, set, GO!" *Give the group 2 minutes to make a tangled knot of their Tethers and then stop action.* [*phase 2*] "Time is over! Now slowly lower your tangled Tethers to the ground and let go. Step away from your tangled Tethers and leave it on the ground. Now walk over to another group's tangled Tethers and pick up the end of a Tether with one hand. Now, without letting go of the Tether, untangle the knot of Tethers." [read the rules below]

Rules

Once you grab the end of the Tether you have to hold on with that same hand until the activity is over.

Starting the game.

Safety Warning

People with shoulder and neck injuries should not participate in this activity.

Story Line

"You are a group of sailors and everyone knows sailors are experts with tying and untying knots in ropes. To keep you sharp and have fun, your captain has created a competition in which small teams must first tie a superior knot and then untie it as fast as possible. Good luck!"

Facilitator Notes

It's ideal to present this game in such a way that the groups don't know they will have to ultimately untangle the Tethers. If the groups realize they will have to untangle the Tethers then they tend to either (a) work really hard at making a tangled mess to hand over to another team or (b) put very little effort in tangling the Tethers. It's better if you just encourage all groups to do the best job they can at tangling the Tethers and once tangled, then you can give the directions about untangling.

Debriefing Suggestions

Are you working with a team that needs to experience what it's like to make a mess and then hand it off to another team to solve? Sometimes you see this in shift workers – they will either create a problem or recognize one and then postpone solving it if they know the next shift will solve it. It's the old "passing the buck" syndrome.

What is perfect about this problem?

What can we do to avoid problems altogether?

What is our responsibility to this problem? Is it ours to solve?

Variations

1. If you have only 6 or 8 people total then you can still lead this activity. Have the group both tangle the Tethers AND untangle their own mess.
2. If your group size is not divisible by 6 then you will have to be creative. You might need to make two teams of 8 (four Tethers required for a group of 8). When it's time to switch, teams of 8 must switch with teams of 8.

3. An alternative to having teams switch and untangle each other's knots is to have the team untangle their own knot.
4. Time the group to untangle the knot.
5. Close your eyes while untying the knot. It takes lots longer but it can be done.

History

I learned this activity from Sam Sikes. Sam calls this activity "Knot Exchange" but I call it "Inhuman Knot" because it reminds me of another teambuilding game called "Human Knot" (described in this book). Find Sam on the web at: **www.doingworks.com**

Related Quote

"A good knot on a bad rope is no better than a bad knot."

~ Alvin Smith

Interference

Group Size: 20 – 100

Age Range: middle school – adult

Intensity: Mental: easy....♦......................hard

Physical: easy....♦......................hard

Time: 10 – 20 minutes (without debrief)

Space: minimal...................♦......lots

Set Up Time: 1 minute

Amount of Duct Tape Required: 40 - 60 feet

View Video: www.DuctTapeTeambuildingGames.com

Username: duct   Password: tape

Game Objective

The group is divided into three teams: Group A, B and C. Group A must communicate a message to Group C so that Group C can repeat the message. Group B must stop the message from being successfully communicated.

Skills Developed

Communication, Process Improvement, Problem Solving, Creativity, Planning, Fun

Set Up / Preparation

1. Prepare three “messages” in advance. Don’t let the participants see these messages yet. Each message will appear on a separate sheet of paper. Suggested messages are:
    - A friend is a present you give yourself.
    - You don’t have to try, you just have to be.
    - The quieter you become the more you can hear.
2. Create the playing area by taping two 20 to 30-feet long sections of duct tape on the ground parallel to each other. The duct tape should be at least 30 feet apart. If the group is large (100+) you will need longer sections of duct tape and the duct tape will need to be farther apart to accommodate the size of the group.
3. Divide the large group into three smaller equal groups. Group A will be the “Message Senders”, Group B will be the “Message Interferers” and Group C will be the “Message Receivers”.

Presenting the Challenge

1. Assign the small groups (A, B and C) to their playing area: Group B (Message Interferers) can stand anywhere between the parallel lines of duct tape. Group A stands on one side of the duct tape line (not between the lines) and Group C stands on the other side of the duct tape lines. Refer to the diagram below.

	I		I	
Group A	I	Group B	I	Group C
	I		I	

2. Presentation Script:
   - [Speaking to Group A] -- "Your challenge is to successfully communicate a message I'm about to provide you to Group C. You'll have only 60 seconds to communicate the message."
   - [Speaking to Group C] -- "Your challenge is to successfully receive the message Group A is going to communicate to you. At the end of 60 seconds you must be able to repeat the exact message I originally gave to Group A."
   - [Speaking to Group B] -- "Your challenge is to prevent Group C from receiving the message. If at the end of 60 seconds Group C is unable to repeat the original message exactly then you will have succeeded."

Rules

1. At the end of 60 seconds, everyone must be silent and Group C will share the message they received. Groups A and C win if it is the exact message sent by Group A. If Group C has only part (or none) of the message, Group B (the message interferers) wins.
2. Only verbal communication may be used to send the message. Communicating the message via written word is not permitted.
3. Each group must stay in their designated playing area (behind their lines). No one may travel beyond the ends of the lines.
4. Everyone must keep their feet on the ground.

Safety Warning

I offer the rule requiring everyone to keep their feet on the ground because some people might want to climb on top of someone's shoulders to get better eye contact (trying to enhance communication). Requiring people to keep their feet on the ground prevents the unsafe practice of people climbing on each other's shoulders or climbing on chairs or tables.

Story Line

"You're a community of people living on one side of a canyon and you must communicate an important message to the community of people living on the other side of the canyon. Every time you attempt to communicate a group of wolves begin howling which interferes with the message. Before time runs out, you must get your message sent and received despite the interference from the wolves."

Facilitator Notes

1. When everything is set and everyone understands the objective and rules, the facilitator will secretly show Group A (the message senders) the message, which is: "A friend is a present you give yourself." Prepare this message ahead of time and write it on white paper using a black marker in large easy to read print. Do not let the other teams see the message! Allow the message senders 30 to 60 seconds to prepare a plan and then start the game! After 60 seconds stop the game so you can hear what Group C (the message receivers) heard. If it is the exact message you supplied to Group A, then Group A and C win.
2. Prepare for round # 2 by asking Group A to move to the center of the playing area where they will now be message interferers. Group B moves to the message receiving area and Group C moves to the message sending area. The message to be sent during round two is: "You don't have to try, you just have to be." Repeat the same process as in the first round.
3. Prepare for round # 3 by asking Group C to move to the center of the playing area where they will now be the message interferers. Group A moves to the message receiving area and Group B moves to the message sending area. The message to be sent during round three is: "The quieter you become the more you can hear."
4. It's important for each group to rotate into each of the positions (sender, interferer, receiver) so that everyone has an experience of each position.
5. The Message Interferers will usually yell like wild animals and direct their yelling at either the Message Senders or the Message Receivers (or both). The Interferers may jump up

and down and wave their arms so as to act as a further distraction.

6. Message Senders who are successful will tend to plan their efforts well and yell their message as a unified group.
7. This activity gets VERY loud. Make sure you won't disturb others when you play this game.

Debriefing Suggestions

After three rounds, ask the group to regroup into smaller discussion groups of 4 or 5 people and then ask these questions:

- What is true about communication?
- What strategies worked well in sending a message? Which of the strategies can you use in real life?
- What strategies that worked well in receiving a message can you use in real life?
- What did you learn/experience about interfering with messages? What is important there to understand?

Usually these questions lead to greater insights and understandings about effective communication. There is always some kind of interference going on; however, this does not mean communication has to stop or be unclear. If the message senders and the message receivers are committed to the process they will overcome most of the interferences.

Variations

1. Create your own one sentence messages for the groups to use during this game.
2. In the standard presentation of this game I am very adament in keeping the messages (sentences) at approximately the same length. Consider giving the third group a message that is double the normal length. You will most probably see resistance from the Message Senders and Receivers. They will perhaps complain that the message is too long and it's unfair. This could create a great opening to discuss topics like fairness, the complexity of the messages we send, new strategies developed to send and receive complex messages, etc.

History

This game was taught to me by master teambuilder Earl Davis of Moonshadow Learning Services **www.moonshadow.net**

Related Quote

"Don't let what you cannot do interfere with what you can do."

~ John Wooden

Jump Rope Record

Group Size: 7 – 15

Age Range: elementary school – adult

Intensity: Mental: easy.........♦................hard

Physical: easy.....................♦....hard

Time: 10 – 20 minutes (without debrief)

Space: minimal...................♦......lots

Set Up Time: 5 minutes

Amount of Duct Tape Required: 100 feet

View Video: www.DuctTapeTeambuildingGames.com

Username: duct Password: tape

Game Objective

The group sets a record by collectively jumping the jump rope as many times as possible.

Skills Developed

Fun, Energizer, Goals

Set Up / Preparation

Create a 25-feet long section of duct tape "rope". It takes three people to create this duct tape rope: one person who dispenses duct tape and two people to hold the ends of the duct tape. Pull off a 25-feet section of duct tape and have two volunteers hold the ends of this piece of duct tape. Repeat this process three more times, allowing all four long pieces of duct tape to stick to each other. Now have the duct tape holders twist the duct tape rope (the four "strands") - this will help bind the four 25-feet long strips of duct tape together to make one duct tape rope. If you can, try to string out the 25-feet long strips of duct tape in such a way that their sticky sides are not exposed (this isn't critical).

Presenting the Challenge

1. Get two volunteers to act as the jump rope turners. Have the group (or a portion of the group) stand on one side of the jump rope which is lying on the floor.
2. Presentation Script: "Your challenge is to collectively jump the jump rope as many times as you can without anyone missing. Your goal is to get the entire team to jump at one time and as many times as possible." [read the rules below]

Rules

1. Turning direction, turning speed and standing direction are up to the group.
2. The group can start with just a few members of the team jumping and then add more team members as skill and confidence grows.

Safety Warning

The larger the group jumping the more likely it is that someone will get bumped or fall into someone else and possibly cause an injury.

Use your good judgment when deciding if the group is too large to attempt the game safely.

Story Line

"You are a team of secret agents who have been hired to rescue a stolen formula for a new kind of duct tape. The formula is being kept in a room that has a high tech alarm system with a laser beam that sweeps the room's floor. Your team must practice jumping the laser beam so you can avoid detection."

Facilitator Notes

If you have a big group (10 to 15 people) this game can get very difficult. If one person jumps at the wrong time it stops the game AND everyone knows who is responsible. The pressure can get intense for someone who keeps getting caught by the rope. Watch for situations where the group might focus their frustration on one person.

Debriefing Suggestions

Because this game requires a coordinated, perfectly timed effort by the entire team, I like to ask the following debrief questions:

What strategies did you use in this game to coordinate your efforts? How many of these same strategies are applicable in your day-to-day life as a team?

What big challenges do you face as a team that truly require a coordinated effort to solve/address?

Variations

Start with two team members at first (rather than the entire team) and see if they can jump successfully together. Then add more team members gradually until the entire team is able to jump together.

History

Karl Rohnke described a variation of this game in his classic teambuilding games book “Silverbullets”. **www.karlrohnke.com**

Related Quote

“The most dangerous strategy is to jump a chasm in two leaps.”

~ Benjamin Disraeli

Key Punch

Group Size: 7 – 20
Age Range: high school – adult
Intensity: Mental: easy..................♦.......hard
Physical: easy..............♦...........hard
Time: 15 – 25 minutes (without debrief)
Space: minimal...................♦......lots
Set Up Time: 5 minutes
Amount of Duct Tape Required: 50 - 70 feet
View Video: www.DuctTapeTeambuildingGames.com
Username: duct Password: tape

Game Objective

Touch all 30 of the numbered duct tape cards in sequence as quickly as possible.

Skills Developed

Communication, Leadership, Roles & Responsibilities, Process Improvement, Problem Solving, Creativity, Planning, Goals

Set Up / Preparation

1. Key Punch Cards: Create 30 "Key Punch Cards". The cards measure 4 x 5 inches (approximately) and are made out of duct tape (see photo below). Using a black marker, number the cards 1 - 30. Consider having your participants make the cards with you as part of the activity. *NOTE: These cards can be used for other games in this book including All My Neighbors and Four Corner Traverse.*

2. Playing Area: Create the playing area by applying duct tape to the ground. First create a giant rectangle measuring approximately 15 feet on the short side and 20 feet on the long side. Next, create the Start / Stop Line about 20 to 40 feet from the rectangle. Spread out all 30 of the numbered Key Punch Cards inside the rectangle. Keep numbers that are next to each other (sequentially) far apart from each other (as best you can) - for example, card # 1 might be on one side of the rectangle and card # 2 on the other side.

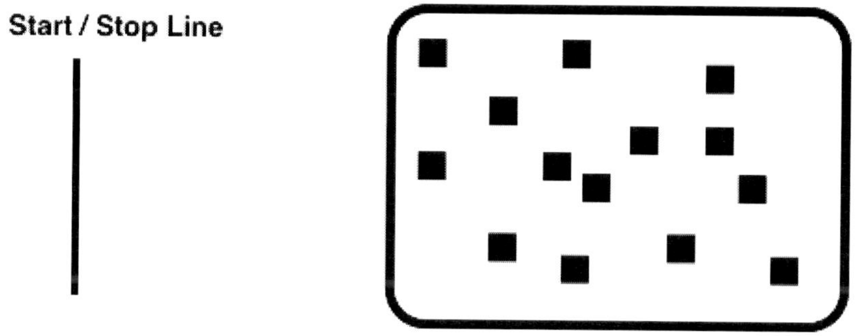

Presenting the Challenge

1. Gather the team behind the Start / Stop Line and read the "Presentation Script" below and then the rules.
2. Presentation Script: "Your challenge is to physically touch all 30 of the numbered cards in sequence (ascending order) as quickly as possible. Your team will have up to five attempts to get the best time possible." [read the rules below]

Rules

1. Time Allotment: Your team has 25 minutes or five attempts, whichever comes first. If the team uses five attempts in 18 minutes, you are done; if the team uses three attempts in 25 minutes, you are done. Time begins when the facilitator says "Go!"
2. The entire team must begin and finish behind the start line. The stopwatch starts as soon as the first person steps over the line. The watch stops when the last person crosses back over the line.
3. Anytime the team or a member of the team crosses the start line, it is considered an attempt.
4. Only one person can be on the keyboard (inside the rectangle) at a time. If two or more people are inside the rectangle simultaneously, a glitch occurs and a penalty time of 10 seconds is added to the score.

5. If any number is touched out of sequence (for example, 3 and then 5), this infraction causes the computer to crash and a penalty time of 10 seconds is added to the score.
6. The team cannot return to the rectangle between attempts in order to study the number set up (or for any other reason).
7. All planning must occur behind the line where the team starts each round. "Scouting trips" are not permitted.
8. The playing area (start/stop line, cards, rectangle, etc.) may not be adjusted or otherwise moved.

Safety Warning

1. People with knee or feet injuries should not play this game.
2. Make sure the Key Punch Cards will not slide around on the playing surface. If the cards slide someone might fall down and get injured. If the cards slide you might be able to tape them to the floor.
3. Because this game encourages fast movement as a team, make sure you have a playing area free of hazards. You don't want people slipping and falling down.

Story Line

"A militant group of computer hackers have introduced a terrible computer virus into many of the major computer systems around the world. If the virus is not stopped soon, all kinds of computer records will be lost or damaged causing major havoc. Your team has been called in to stop this virus before it's too late. To stop the virus your team must touch all of the 30 keys (cards) on the giant computer keyboard in order as fast as you can. If your score is low enough you will stop the virus from spreading. Good luck!"

Facilitator Notes

1. I like to provide the group with a written set of directions for this activity although this is not necessary for the successful conduct of the game.
2. For the first attempt, the group will usually send one person in to touch all the Key Punch Cards with the rest of the group standing along the outside of the rectangle pointing to the next

card in sequence. To get the lowest possible time, however, the group will need to work together and share the responsibility of touching the cards. Though much more difficult because of the coordination of efforts, the results (the time) will be better.

3. During the activity I fill in the data gathered during the activity in the "Key Punch Facilitator Record Keeping" log (see below). This data can be used in the debrief (see below). If you have a co-facilitator, it's best if one of you is responsible for data collection and the other focuses on the process.

Key Punch Facilitator Record Keeping Log

Attempt	Time Attempt was Initiated	Time w/o penalties	Penalties @ 10 sec. each	Total Time (Time + Penalty Time)
1				
2				
3				
4				
5				

Debriefing Suggestions

1. The Key Punch is a great activity to discuss "continuous improvement". Did the group use the same strategy with each attempt or did they come up with new ones? Were the new ideas executed well? What is the relationship between a good idea and the execution of that idea? How were new ideas handled by the group?
2. During the activity I fill in the data gathered in the "Key Punch Facilitator Record Keeping" log and I use this data during the debrief period of the activity. Depending on the sophistication level of the group, I'll hand the record keeping log over to the group and ask them to analyze the data and interpret it and then deliver a presentation based on their findings.
3. A TRUE STORY: I worked for the YMCA for five years as a senior program director and along the way I became a faculty

level trainer for the YMCA of the USA leading a two-day management module called "Group Work" for YMCA professionals. During this training I would lead the Key Punch activity for the workshop attendees. A common occurrence was for the group to pick one person (usually someone fast and young) to run into the rectangle and touch all the cards by himself or herself, with the rest of the team standing on the outside pointing. After the fifth attempt at touching all the cards by themselves, this person was always exhausted. This presented a great opening to discuss the relationship between working hard and working smart (i.e. working as a team). In the mid 90's when I was leading this workshop, the average YMCA professional staff person lasted two years at their job and then they moved on. After leading this workshop and the Key Punch activity I began to get a sense of why the burnout rate was so high - people who work for the YMCA (as well as other non-profits) have such a strong desire to make a difference in the lives of others that many forget to take care of themselves. Their approach to work is unsustainable over the long period. By participating in the Key Punch activity, YMCA staff would have an opportunity to see and experience their behavior and discuss alternatives that would support them in the long term.

Variations

1. Ask the team to simply surround the rectangle. Then ask them to touch all 30 cards in sequence as quickly as possible. They can stand around the rectangle and discuss strategies.
2. Have the same number of Key Punch Cards as you have team members (for instance, 15 people & 15 cards). Assign each person a number. See how long it takes the group to touch all 15 numbers in sequence. Similar rules as the "regular" Key Punch activity (start outside the rectangle, only one person is allowed inside the rectangle at a time, etc.).
3. If you have a group of 16 people, have them pair up. Set out 16 numbers inside the rectangle. Assign a number to each person. Have the group attempt to touch all of the 16 numbers in sequence with the following rules: only one person allowed inside the rectangle at a time, anyone inside the rectangle must keep his eyes closed and his partner is to guide him to the number using only voice commands (the partner is not allowed inside the rectangle), when the number is touched they must keep their eyes closed and walk out of the circle and the next person can go in. No penalty for touching numbers out of sequence (though you must touch YOUR number).
4. Instead of writing numbers on the spots, write out the alphabet. Supply your team with a word or phrase that they must spell out by touching the correct card (letter) in order.

History

This game was described in the classic teambuilding games book *Quicksilver* by Karl Rohnke and Steve Butler.
www.karlrohnke.com

Related Quote

"Love is the master key which opens the gates of happiness."

~ Oliver Wendell Holmes

Make A Machine

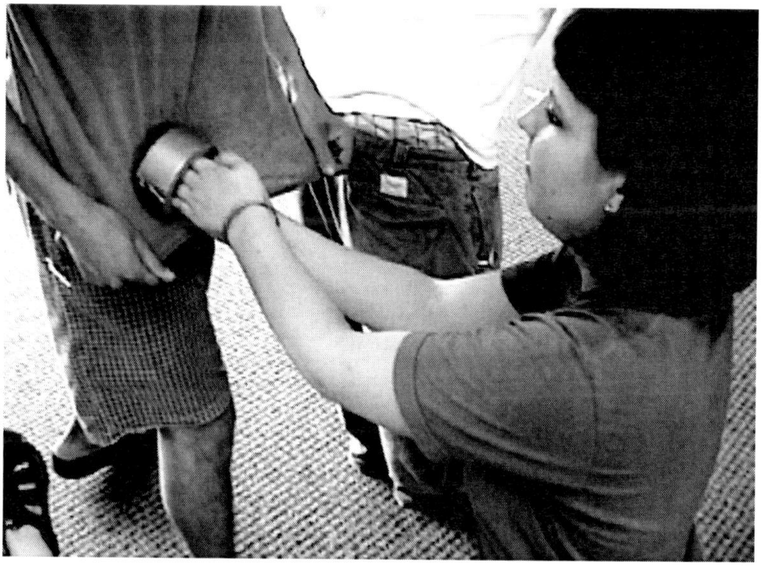

Group Size: 4 – 15
Age Range: elementary school – adult
Intensity: Mental: easy....♦......................hard
Physical: easy.....♦....................hard
Time: 5 – 10 minutes (without debrief)
Space: minimal....♦.....................lots
Set Up Time: 1 minute
Amount of Duct Tape Required: 1 roll of duct tape per group
View Video: www.DuctTapeTeambuildingGames.com
Username: duct Password: tape

Game Objective

Manufacture (imaginatively) a roll of duct tape.

Skills Developed

Communication, Planning

Set Up / Preparation

1. You'll need one roll of duct tape for this activity but you won't be pulling any of the duct tape off the roll.
2. Gather the team in a circle and present the challenge.

Presenting the Challenge

1. In this challenge the group will work collaboratively and imaginatively to create a "machine" that will produce/create one roll of duct tape.
2. Presentation Script: "Your challenge is to create a machine that will create a roll of duct tape. Each person on the team will act as a component of the machine. Be creative." [read the rules below]

Rules

1. The first component of the duct tape machine must include some sort of button that the facilitator can push to start the machine.
2. The last component of the machine must deliver the roll of duct tape to the facilitator.
3. Every member of the team must be included in the machine in some way.
4. Your team will earn bonus points for creativity.
5. You can/cannot [facilitator decides] utilize props from your surroundings.
6. Your team must have a completed machine in five minutes and be ready to demonstrate your machine in action.

Safety Warning

Be safe throughout this activity. It can be dangerous around manufacturing plants.

Story Line

“There is a massive shortage in duct tape and your team must quickly create a duct tape manufacturing plant. By creatively assembling your team into a duct tape making machine you’ll save the day!”

Facilitator Notes

To play this game well (to be very creative) requires a deep level of vulnerability based trust. There is a direct correlation between deep trust and high creativity.

Creativity and innovation are absolutely critical to a team’s success. To get more insights into this topic listen to the free audio interview with innovation expert Thomas Koulopoulos at:

www.TeachMeTeamwork.com

To find the audio interview click on “Audio Interviews” in the right hand column or type the following web address into your browser’s address bar:

http://tinyurl.com/5ggpxn

Debriefing Suggestions

In this game your team collectively created (manufactured) a roll of duct tape using your imagination and teamwork.

To what degree do you believe we can use the same creative process to create a new reality (future) for your team?

Variations

Divide your group into multiple teams and have these teams compete with each other to develop the most creative duct tape manufacturing plant.

History

This game was taught to me by master teambuilder Jeff Long.

Related Quote

""Winners make a habit of manufacturing their own positive expectations in advance of the event." ~ **Brian Tracy**

Maze

Group Size: 4 – 15
Age Range: middle school – adult
Intensity: Mental: easy...................♦......hard
Physical: easy...♦......................hard
Time: 20 – 30 minutes (without debrief)
Space: minimal..................♦......lots
Set Up Time: 5 minutes
Amount of Duct Tape Required: approximately 80 feet
View Video: www.DuctTapeTeambuildingGames.com
Username: duct Password: tape

Game Objective

Your team must successfully solve the established yet hidden Maze route and get as many team members through the Maze before time runs out.

Skills Developed

Communication, Roles & Responsibilities, Problem Solving

Set Up / Preparation

1. Create a "Maze" by creating a 4 x 4 grid (16 boxes) on the ground out of duct tape. To create this grid you'll need ten 8-feet long strips of duct tape. When you're done, each box in the grid should be approximately 2 x 2 feet. Your grid should look something like this:

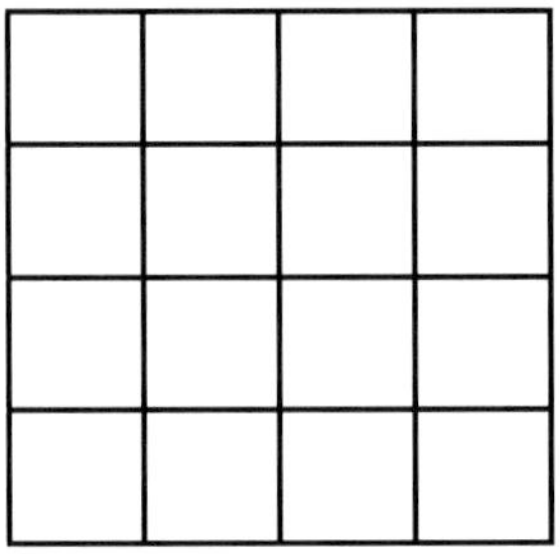

2. Create a "Maze Map" (answer key) for the facilitator to reference during the game. As the group members travel through the Maze, the facilitator will compare their movement with the Maze Map. The Maze Map can be printed on a piece of paper and will look something like this:

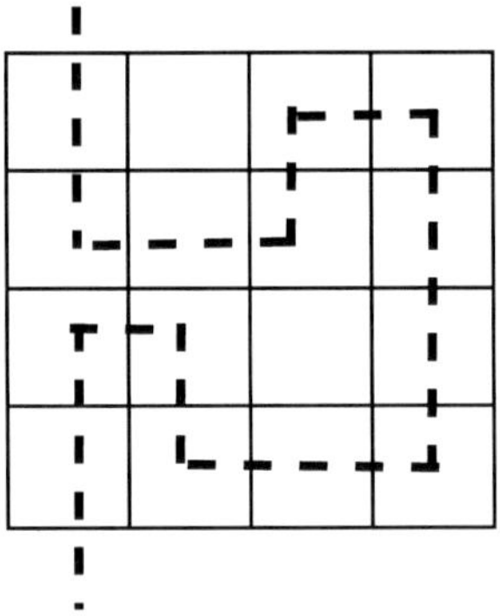

Presenting the Challenge

1. Make the group stand on one side of the Maze (start side) and you (the facilitator) stand on the other side of the Maze (the ending side).
2. Presenting the Directions: When presenting this Maze activity, you can choose to read the directions to the group or you can supply them with a copy of the written directions. Older participants (high school age and older) tend to be able to make sense of the directions without much help from the facilitator. Younger participants (elementary and middle school age) may have difficulty deciphering exactly what they are supposed to do. With younger participants you may need to help them work through the directions, section by section and rule by rule, so they have a clear understanding – this may take 10-15 minutes.
3. Presentation Script: "Your challenge is to solve the established yet hidden Maze route AND get as many of your team members through the Maze before time runs out. There is one route through the Maze and I will compare your movements through the Maze with my "Maze Map" (answer key). You must follow all the rules." [read the rules below]

Facilitator holding the Maze map.

Rules

1. Your team must begin and end the Maze at the areas specified by the facilitator.
2. There is one route through the Maze and the facilitator has a "map" of the route (answer key). The group must establish a sequence and each person must attempt the route in the established order. After each person in the entire group has made an attempt, the order starts over.
3. There can be only one person on the Maze at a time.
4. If a correct square has been stepped on, there will be silence from the facilitator. If an incorrect square is stepped on, the facilitator will make a "beep" sound. When an individual hears the "beep", he must leave the Maze and wait for his turn again.
5. When the first person on the team steps onto the Maze, no further verbal communication will be allowed. The team must notify the facilitator when the first person is about to step onto the Maze.
6. Team members may only keep mental records of the Maze route (no marking the route or drawing of maps, etc.).
7. The Maze may not be altered in anyway.
8. Violation of a rule may result in a penalty (time may be reduced, someone might have to wear a blind fold, etc.).
9. Time Allotment: Your team has 25 minutes to complete the objective.

Safety Warning

This activity is fairly safe unless you lead it in a pit filled with poisonous snakes (not advised).

Story Line

"Your team has traveled back in time to find a plant that may hold the key to curing a deadly disease. You've found the plant and must now get your team and the plant back through the Time Maze to return to the present time and save the world!"

Facilitator Notes

1. The average group needs 25 minutes to complete the challenge (if they are working well together). As a point of reference, a group of 15 ten year olds can usually solve the Maze in 25 minutes (getting everyone through) if the facilitator uses the Maze Map provided.
2. The group is allowed to talk only during the planning phase of this activity. Once the first person steps on the Maze, verbal communication is prohibited. The group is allowed to use non-verbal communication (ex. pointing).
3. As team members move through the Maze, your job is to match their movements with those of the answer key (Maze map). If a participant steps on the wrong square, you will say, "BEEP". The person who was "beeped" must get off the Maze and let the next person go (the beeped person goes again when it's their turn). I've found that the best place to position yourself during this activity is at the end opposite to where the participants started.
4. Some facilitators find it difficult to both watch the group AND watch where the individual moving through the Maze is stepping AND comparing this individual's movement to that of the answer key. Consider having an assistant whose job it is to operate the answer key (Maze Map).
5. Once someone makes it through the Maze successfully, they do not have to go through again. They should now focus on helping everyone else get through.
6. A general rule is to provide the group with approximately 25 minutes of time to complete this challenge. With this amount of time a group can usually get the entire group through the Maze when using a simple Maze Map is being used.
7. If the group violates any of the rules you can penalize the group by taking away activity time (for example, one instance of talking during the activity means on minute less time to complete the activity).
8. With a difficult Maze Map, this activity becomes intensely team focused – there just isn't a way to complete the activity in time without working well as a team.

9. One of the things I like most about this activity is that I can easily vary the difficulty level of the activity to match the needs of the group.

Debriefing Suggestions

I use this activity to teach a number of important lessons. Here are some questions and topics that you can choose to pursue with the group after the activity.

1. Who solved the Maze? This is a tricky question. This does not ask who the first person through the Maze was; yet some groups see the first person through as the person who "solved" the puzzle. The reality is that it took everyone's effort to get the first person through.
2. Who received help from others during the activity? Who gave help? Some participants are reluctant to either give or receive help. This question can start a great discussion about the topic of helping others. It can also lead into a conversation about trust - who did you trust to give you information and advice during this activity? Did anyone receive advice (directions) that led them to make an incorrect move? How do you know who to trust in the real world? What criteria do you have to trust someone?
3. Who made a mistake during this activity? Everyone will make a mistake at some point during this activity. When everyone acknowledges that they all made mistakes I point out that they were still able to solve the challenge (if in fact they were able to). I then ask the group to tell me whether mistakes are "good" or "bad". Generally groups will say that mistakes are good when you pay attention to them and don't repeat them; and they are bad when the same mistake is repeated over and over again.

Variations

1. You can vary the difficulty by decreasing the amount of time (less time makes it harder). You can also increase the difficulty level by using a more complex Maze Map. A more difficult Maze Map has a route that is longer and has more turns and might include diagonal moves.

2. One way to make this activity easier is to allow the group to move away from the Maze and meet in a "special" meeting area (for example, inside a rope circle) to talk freely. During this time you can stop the clock. Doing this encourages problem solving and sharing of ideas.
3. A funny and challenging variation is to divide the group in half and ask the two small groups to travel through the Maze in opposite directions. Will they help each other?
4. Consider penalizing the group for stepping in squares that are wrong AND where they've stepped more than once. This will cause the group to slow down and pay close attention to NOT repeating errors.

History

This game was taught to me by master teambuilder Viva Pizer.

Related Quote

"Happiness, that grand mistress of the ceremonies in the dance of life, impels us through all its mazes and meanderings, but leads none of us by the same route." ~ **Charles Caleb Colton**

Minefield

Group Size: 4 – 30
Age Range: middle school – adult
Intensity: Mental: easy................♦........hard
Physical: easy.....♦....................hard
Time: 15 – 30 minutes (without debrief)
Space: minimal..................♦......lots
Set Up Time: 7 minutes
Amount of Duct Tape Required: 40 - 60 feet
View Video: www.DuctTapeTeambuildingGames.com
Username: duct Password: tape

Game Objective

Travel through the minefield with the help of your partner.

Skills Developed

Trust, Communication, Planning

Set Up / Preparation

1. Create the playing area. For a group of 12 people, start by creating a 10 ft x 10 ft square on the ground out of duct tape (larger groups need a larger size playing area). On the "start" and "finish" sides of the box create "doors" using 6-inch long strips of duct tape - these short pieces of duct tape need to be two feet apart (refer to the diagram below).

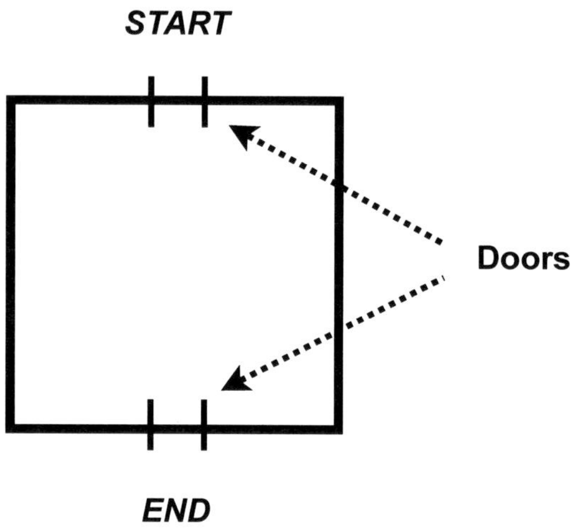

2. Create obstacles (land mines) in the playing area by filling the square (playing area) with pieces of duct tape. The more obstacles you add the harder the game will be. Adding approximately 30 pieces of duct tape into the square will provide a medium level of difficulty for most groups. The duct tape pieces can be made in several ways. To make reusable duct tape pieces simply pull off four to five inch long sections of duct tape and fold them over (fold the sticky side onto itself). This makes a little square shape you can use over and over. You can also make duct tape obstacles (land mines) by pulling

off five to six inch long pieces of duct tape and make a circle so the sticky side is facing out. Place these sticky-side-out duct tape circles (pieces) on their edge (standing up) or on their sides inside the playing area. Spread out the obstacles in such a way that there are no straight pathways through the minefield.

> NOTE: During the actual activity, you may find that the group has located an easy pathway which you did not see until the game has started. I allow myself the option to change/adjust the minefield playing area midstream by rearranging the obstacles. If the group challenges me on this I usually say I'm attempting to mimic real life in that things change and you can either adapt or complain.

Presenting the Challenge

1. Have everyone find a partner and stand on the "start" side of the square playing area.
2. <u>Presentation Script:</u> "Your challenge is to travel through the playing area to the other side of the square. You'll be working in teams of two. At the beginning of the game everyone will start behind the line on the "start" side of the square. Teams of two (partners) can work independently of other teams. When traveling through the playing area (minefield) your eyes must be closed which means your partner must coach you / guide you (verbally) through the minefield helping you avoid the obstacles (land mines). When the first person in your partnership makes it to the other side he/she can open his/her eyes and the rolls switch - now that person becomes the coach and guides his/her partner (verbally) through the playing area from the start side to the end side." [read the rules below]

Rules

1. No running or fast moving.
2. People must stand behind the start line or the end line or be walking through the playing area (minefield). No one is allowed on the sides of the playing area.
3. Anyone inside the playing area must have his/her eyes closed.
4. More than two people can be inside the playing area.

5. You must enter and exit through one of the “doors”.
6. If anyone touches a land mine or the perimeter of the playing area, they must return to the start side and try again.
7. The participants may not alter the playing area but the facilitator can.
8. Violation of a rule may result in a penalty.

Safety Warning

1. The playing area must be safe because people will be walking around with their eyes closed. Make sure the playing area is level and flat.
2. If someone needs to open his eyes to feel safe that’s fine.

Story Line

“To escape a pack of wild hamsters your team must travel through a strange tunnel that’s filled with an odd gas which, if it makes contact with your eyes, will make you cry uncontrollably. Therefore you must work in pairs to travel through the tunnel - one partner coaches the other who walks through the tunnel with his/her eyes closed. Be careful not to step on the hamster droppings (pieces of duct tape) while in the tunnel!”

Facilitator Notes

1. If you have an uneven number of people just create one team of 3 (Person A, Person B, Person C). Person A goes through the playing area first, then coaches Person B through who coaches Person C through.
2. I've led this activity effectively with groups as small as 4 people and as large as 80. The great thing about this activity is people work in pairs and can be somewhat independent of the other people.
3. When the activity is in full motion, there will be lots of talking and things can get loud (larger groups get louder). With large groups it can feel somewhat chaotic (mostly because of the noise) because multiple teams are working simultaneously.
4. This is a wonderful activity to practice coaching (coaching others and being coached). Every moment of this activity provides ample opportunity to practice clear and precise communication.
5. Once the first person makes it to the other side he/she will typically only coach his/her partner through. However, that same person may choose guide people other than his/her partner. I've deliberately provided rules that allow teams/ people to collaborate.

Debriefing Suggestions

Land mines (obstacles) are metaphoric problems the group faces either personally or as a team. They are everywhere in life (personal & public). Some land mines are big and some are small - - they all do damage when we hit them. In this exercise, there are lots of land mines separating the participants from their desired outcomes (goals).

Life is full of obstacles. Some people allow obstacles to prevent them from succeeding. Others keep running into the obstacles. What are the obstacles in your life (in your team) that you must recognize and then avoid?

We can go through life trying to avoid the obstacles but it's easier when we have help. Where do you get help in real life? Are you effective at asking for help? How good are you at receiving help? How do you know? Are you good at giving help? How do you know?

Variations

1. Provide the team with a time limit. For example, the team has 20 minutes to get the entire team from one side to the other.
2. At the beginning of the activity, before the group actually starts (but after you've supplied the instructions), warn them that a "communication breakdown" may occur during the activity. If this happens, people will not be allowed to communicate verbally. Don't tell them how long it will last (make it last no more than 60 seconds). This will allow people to plan (or not) for this possibility.
3. Provide each person with one index card and have everyone write down an attribute they bring to the team on their card. These cards will then be scattered (writing side down) throughout the playing area (inside the square) among the pieces of duct tape obstacles. During the game each person is to pick up ONE card while traveling through the playing area (while remaining sightless) and carry it to the other side. The metaphor here is that everyone brings talents and skills to the team and yet we must work together to bring forth and utilize these talents.
4. Divide the team in half. Group A will start on one side of the playing area and Group B will start on the other side of the playing area. Follow the basic set of rules with this one twist -

- Group A must move to where Group B is and Group B must move to where Group A is (teams moving in opposite directions). Make sure people in Group A partner up with each other and people in Group B partner up with each other. Hopefully the two groups will realize that the game runs better if they collaborate.

5. In the basic setup of this game I provide two "doors" - one at the start and one at the end of the playing area. For larger groups you may need to not only create a larger playing area (square) but may add more doors.

History

This teambuilding game was described by Karl Rohnke in his famous book "Quicksilver" published in 1995.
www.karlrohnke.com

Related Quote

"Faith means living with uncertainty - feeling your way through life, letting your heart guide you like a lantern in the dark"

~ Dan Millman

Partner Walk

Group Size: groups of 2 (pairs)
Age Range: elementary school – adult
Intensity: Mental: easy....♦.....................hard
Physical: easy..............♦...........hard
Time: 5 – 10 minutes (without debrief)
Space: minimal...................♦......lots
Set Up Time: 5 minutes
Amount of Duct Tape Required: 10 - 50 feet depending on the size of the group
View Video: www.DuctTapeTeambuildingGames.com
Username: duct Password: tape

Game Objective

Walk with your partner from one point to another.

Skills Developed

Fun, Energizer

Set Up / Preparation

This game is best played when participants are wearing long pants and tennis shoes.

Presenting the Challenge

1. Have everyone find a partner. Partners should be the same height (approximately).
2. Have partners stand next to each other (side by side) and then ask them to use duct tape to connect adjoining legs - taping in two places: above the ankle and below the knee.
3. Presentation Script: "Your challenge is to walk with your partner around the playing area. Try walking at different speeds and turning. Do not run into other people." [read the rules below]

Rules

1. Partners must walk carefully.
2. No running into other people.

Safety Warning

1. People with knee, ankle or hip injuries should not play this game.
2. Play on a flat surface that is free from any hazards that might trip participants or otherwise cause them to fall down.
3. Participants must be wearing long pants and have tennis shoes on.
4. Do not put duct tape on skin.
5. The faster people move in this game the greater the chance of injury.

6. Duct tape can damage some clothing. If you suspect the duct tape will damage the clothing of the participants do not lead this game.
7. Make sure partners have similar leg length. Do not pair up a short person with a tall person.

Story Line

"On the planet of Ductapicus they determine someone's capacity to work in harmony with another using this "Partner Walk" game. This is your big chance to prove you can work harmoniously with another!"

Facilitator Notes

This is a fun teambuilding game that the gives participants a feeling of what it means to move in harmony with another person.

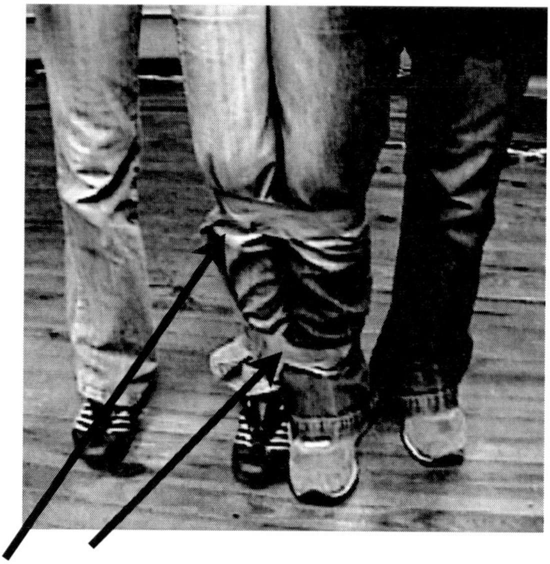

Duct Tape

Debriefing Suggestions

On the surface this game looks like all fun and games but there are powerful lessons just beneath the surface.

Describe what it felt like when you and your partner were moving in sync.

When is it most beneficial for the team / organization to move in sync?

What does it take to get a team to move in sync?

When is it most appropriate to be “out of step” with the team?

Variations

1. Once a team of two is confident at walking, they can try speeding up.
2. Create a team of three. Make sure this group ONLY walks (no running).

History

This game was taught to me by my physical education teacher in elementary school. He had us tie our legs together with rope but duct tape works better.

Related Quote

"Beauty of style and harmony and grace and good rhythm depends on simplicity." ~ **Plato**

Pass the Roll

Group Size: 5 – 15
Age Range: elementary school – adult
Intensity: Mental: easy...♦......................hard
Physical: easy.....♦....................hard
Time: 5 minutes (without debrief)
Space: minimal.......♦..................lots
Set Up Time: 1 minute
Amount of Duct Tape Required: One roll (no tape pulled off though)
View Video: www.DuctTapeTeambuildingGames.com
Username: duct Password: tape

Game Objective

Pass the roll of duct tape around the circle.

Skills Developed

Planning, Patience, Problem Solving, Process Improvement

Set Up / Preparation

Get one roll of duct tape and gather your group together.

Presenting the Challenge

1. Ask your team to sit on the ground in a circle.
2. Presentation Script: "Your challenge is to pass this roll of duct tape around the circle using your feet. If the roll of duct tape touches the ground you must start over." [read the rules below]

Rules

1. Only feet can be used to pass the roll of duct tape.
2. The duct tape is allowed to touch feet only.
3. Each person on the team must participate in the passing of the roll of duct tape.

Safety Warning

People with knee, ankle or back injuries should not participate.

Story Line

"You're a group of aliens with no arms. In your culture it's important to practice passing on the secrets of how the universe is held together (duct tape!). Sit in a circle and pass the roll of duct tape around the circle using your feet only."

Facilitator Notes

This activity is easy and fun to lead. Younger participants (age 8 or 9) will typically have more trouble passing the roll of duct tape than adults. This is a fun, introductory type of activity to lead with a group.

Debriefing Suggestions

I typically don't debrief this activity. I play it as a fun warm up teambuilding game. If you feel compelled to debrief, perhaps you can use this activity as an opening to discuss the team's effectiveness at passing on information or useful tools (rather than hoarding or ignoring).

Variations

1. Try passing the roll of duct tape with your eyes closed.
2. Pass a small ball made out of duct tape around the circle using feet (or toes) only.
3. Pass the roll of duct tape around the circle as fast as you can (time the group). Now try to beat that time and set a "new world record!"

History

This activity was taught to me by master games leader Elbert Hargrave.

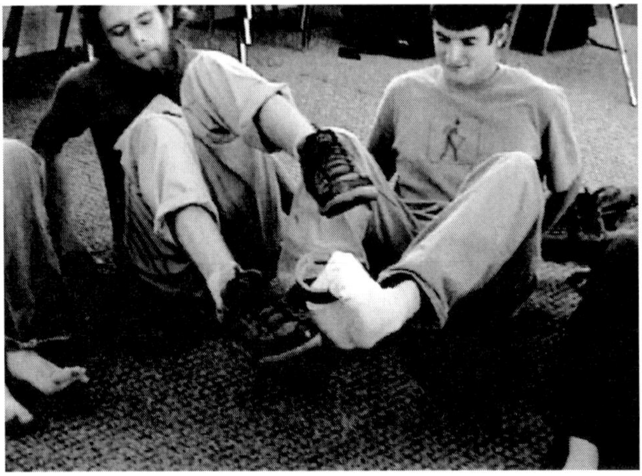

Related Quote

"Live each season as it passes; breathe the air, drink the drink, taste the fruit, and resign yourself to the influences of each."

~ Henry David Thoreau

Photo Finish

Group Size: 6 – 20
Age Range: high school – adult
Intensity: Mental: easy....................♦.....hard
Physical: easy....♦.....................hard
Time: 10 – 30 minutes (without debrief)
Space: minimal...........♦..............lots
Set Up Time: 1 minute
Amount of Duct Tape Required: 15 - 20 feet
View Video: www.DuctTapeTeambuildingGames.com
Username: duct Password: tape

Game Objective

The group must cross the finish line at exactly the same time.

Skills Developed

Clear Communication, Planning, Patience, Problem Solving, Leadership

Set Up / Preparation

Create a finish line (a straight line) on the ground by taping a section of duct tape to the ground. The finish line must be long enough to accommodate the team standing shoulder to shoulder along the line (a little longer is better).

Presenting the Challenge

1. Ask the group to stand on one side of the finish line.
2. Presentation Script: "Your challenge is to cross the finish line as a team AT EXACTLY THE SAME TIME. You cross the finish line when you break the vertical plane of the finish line. The facilitator is the judge. If anyone crosses the finish line before or after the rest of the group you must try again." [read the rules below]

Rules

1. The group has 15 minutes to make 5 attempts at crossing the finish line (breaking the vertical plane of the finish line) at exactly the same time. If the group uses only 3 attempts in 15 minutes they are done. If the group uses 5 attempts in 9 minutes they are done.
2. Each time someone breaks the plane of the finish line the facilitator will say "Click!" (the sound of a "photo finish" camera) which lets the group know an attempt was completed. The facilitator will notify the group if they succeeded in crossing the finish line simultaneously - if they didn't, the group keeps trying.

Safety Warning

Groups typically approach this activity in a slow and methodical way which keeps things safe. Discourage the group from running at the finish line to reduce the likelihood of injury while making it easier for the facilitator to determine if the group crosses simultaneously. To prevent the group from running at the finish line simply place the finish line on the ground near a wall (with the participants back to the wall).

Story Line

"An eccentric wealthy entrepreneur has approached your team with an offer - if you can demonstrate that your team is unified in purpose and direction then the entrepreneur will donate one million dollars to the charity of your choice. The entrepreneur has created a challenge to determine whether your team is in fact unified in purpose and direction: you must cross a finish line at exactly the same time. There are cameras focused on the finish line to verify whether you have succeeded. You have up to 5 attempts to use in 15 minutes. Good luck!"

Facilitator Notes

1. The facilitator should place himself/herself at the end of the line and CAREFULLY watch for anyone crossing the vertical plane of the finish line.
2. Unfortunately, this activity requires you (the facilitator) to act as the line judge. This is unfortunate because the group may become convinced they crossed the finish line simultaneously when they didn't. It can become a battle of wills. The group

must have enough trust and faith in you to make the right judgment or this game won't go over well.

3. It's likely that someone in the group will inadvertently cross the plane of the finish line. Should this happen, you (the facilitator) must say "Click!" and this will represent one of the 5 attempts. Hopefully the group will take greater care around the finish line.

Debriefing Suggestions

Because this activity emphasizes a team's ability to move (take action) in unison, I often follow this activity up with questions about the team's real life action plan(s). Does everyone know what it is? Is everyone invested in the action plan? Are we all moving as one or are we taking action on our own?

Variations

1. To increase the difficulty of this activity simply back the group up against a wall and place the finish line three feet away from the wall. This tactic makes it much more difficult to have an effective meeting to share ideas and strategies.
2. Consider using a digital camera during this game. Take a picture of each attempt (each "Click!"). This can help validate your ruling.

History

This game was taught to me by Jim Cain who coauthored "Teamwork & Teamplay" and Jim learned this game from Sam Sikes who authored "Raptor" and other teambuilding games books.

Related Quote

"Peace is not the product of a victory or a command. It has no finishing line, no final deadline, no fixed definition of achievement. Peace is a never-ending process, the work of many decisions."

~ Oscar Hammerstein

Rescue Litter

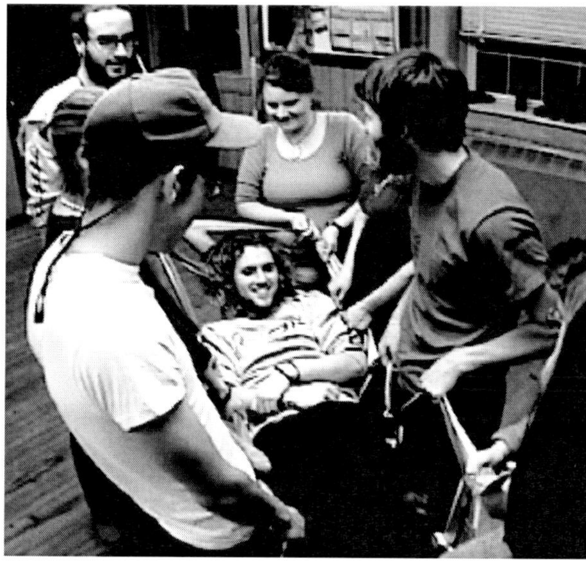

Group Size: 7 – 12
Age Range: high school – adult
Intensity: <u>Mental</u>: easy.................♦.......hard
<u>Physical</u>: easy................♦........hard
Time: 20 – 40 minutes (without debrief)
Space: minimal.............♦...........lots
Set Up Time: 5 minutes
Amount of Duct Tape Required: 60 - 80 feet
View Video: www.DuctTapeTeambuildingGames.com
Username: duct Password: tape

Game Objective

Build a Rescue Litter (stretcher) out of duct tape and use it to safely carry a team member (patient).

Skills Developed

Trust, Leadership, Problem Solving, Creativity, Planning, Resource Management

Set Up / Preparation

1. Read the Safety Warnings (below) before attempting this activity.
2. The ideal place to lead this activity is over a flat, cushioned floor. This will help reduce the likelihood of injuries. The next best place is a grass field.

Presenting the Challenge

1. Gather the team and supply them with a roll of high quality duct tape.
2. <u>Presentation Script:</u> "Your challenge is to build a well designed and constructed Rescue Litter (stretcher) out of duct tape that can be used to safely carry a patient (one of your team members)." [read the rules below]

Rules

1. The Rescue Litter must be well designed and constructed.
2. Once the Rescue Litter is completed, the facilitator will inspect it for safety.
3. Before the patient can be carried, the team must select a leader whose job is to coordinate all lifting. The leader will stand at the right front (head position) of the patient.
4. The team must follow the "How to Lift & Move the Rescue Litter" instructions (below).

Safety Warning

1. Participants with back injuries, arm/shoulder, or leg/knee/foot injuries should not participate in this activity.
2. It is VERY important to use high quality, high strength (expensive) duct tape for this activity. Cheap (inexpensive)

duct tape is more likely to rip or fall apart during the game and thus injur the person being carried.

3. Before you lead this teambuilding game make sure your group is ready for it. They must be strong enough (physically), have a high degree of trust, and should have both a desire and the skills to take care of each other. Do not attempt this game if even one member of the group isn't up to the task.
4. Pay close attention to the team as they build the Rescue Litter. Make sure the Rescue Litter is being built safely and with care. If you see something in the way they're building that makes you uncomfortable stop the game and make sure the team addresses your concerns.
5. Do not attempt this activity with fewer than 7 people - one carried in the Rescue Litter (a patient) and six carriers (lifters).
6. Teach everyone how to lift the Rescue Litter safely (see below).
7. Whenever a patient is being carried, one person must be assigned to the head-neck area of the patient (stands at the top of the Rescue Litter near the head). This head-neck person is in charge of safety and makes sure all lifters are focused and coordinated in their efforts and also makes sure the head-neck of the patient is treated gently.

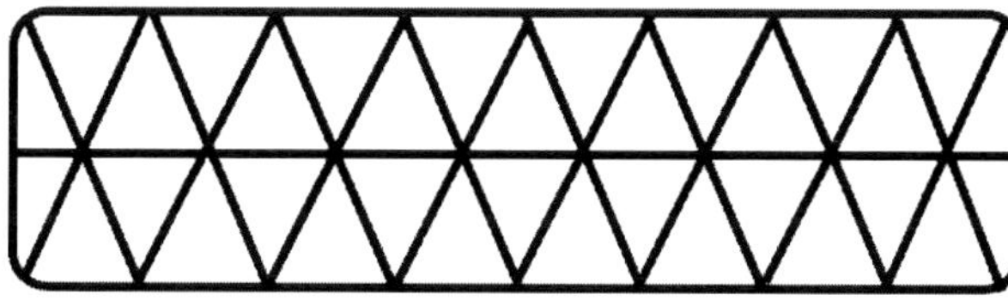

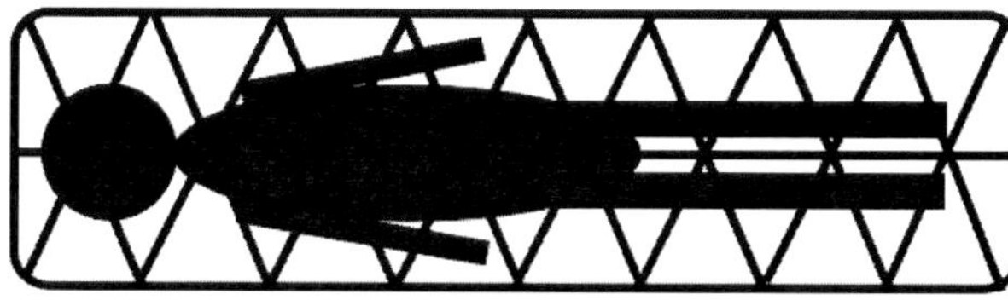

How to Lift & Move the Rescue Litter

Litter Lifting

1. Six to eight individuals line up on alongside the litter (three or four per side); the person at the right front (head position) is in charge of the lift. All individuals get down on one knee facing the litter.
2. Once the patient is in the litter and secured, the team must bring the litter to waist height to begin transport.
3. Grab the litter “rail” with both hands.
4. On the command "lift to the knees," straighten your back and lift with both hands, pulling the litter up to knee height.
5. On the command "lift to the waist," use your rear leg to lever yourself to a standing position, with both hands still on the litter.

Litter Carry

1. After the litter is lifted, the team leader commands 'face front.' At this point take your front hand off the litter and rotate your body to face the front (head) of the litter.
2. On the command 'forward', start walking with your inside foot first. Ideally, the people on each side of the litter are 'out of step with each other,' to avoid bouncing the litter, but moving the litter should not be stopped merely to stay in step.
3. If you tire and need relief, alert the team leader. A relief bearer will come up directly behind you and grab the litter. When he tells you that he has 'got the litter' you may let go and move off to the side. At this point you join the pool of relief bearers.

Setting The Litter Down

1. To set the litter down, the team leader calls a halt and then says 'face center.' At this point the bearers rotate their bodies to face the litter and grab the litter rails with both hands.
2. The team leader then commands 'lower to the knees.' At this point keep your back straight and lower yourself to a

kneeling position with the litter in front of you and at knee height.

3. On the command 'lower to the ground,' bend forward slightly until the litter is safely on the ground.

Story Line

"Your team has been called upon to carry an injured hiker out of the wilderness. Luckily you have a roll of duct tape to build a Rescue Litter!"

Facilitator Notes

1. Groups usually find it easier to build the Rescue Litter in the air / while holding it up (vs. on the ground).
2. Encourage the group to build the Rescue Litter in such a way that the sticky side of the tape is not exposed. This helps prevent hair and skin from getting stuck to the duct tape.
3. Consider having the group design the Rescue Litter on paper before building it. You can approve the design before they build. This may help conserve duct tape. An alternative is to provide the group with the design (see below) and have the group build the Rescue Litter using the supplied design.

Debriefing Suggestions

Carrying a team member (patient) in a litter can be a very empowering teambuilding event. People usually realize that the patient is vulnerable (while being carried) and, therefore, the team must work together well to protect the patient. The patient - caregiver relationship tends to open up windows for conversations that are new and unique for the team:

- How does the design and construction of the Rescue Litter reflect on how we've designed and constructed our team / organization?
- Describe what it was like to be carried (to be the patient) in the Rescue Litter. What did you like about how the team worked together that you would like to see repeated every day?
- Those who acted as the Rescue Litter leader must describe their experience. What did they learn about leading the team

that can help shed light on how the team functions under any situation?

Variations

1. If you're concerned about your group's ability to safely carry a team member but still want your team to experience the Rescue Litter game, find a life-size mannequin to carry.
2. Have the team transport the patient through, over and around obstacles.
3. Require the team to rotate the position of patient (person being carried) so that everyone gets a chance to be carried.

History

During my training as a Wilderness First Responder I was introduced to building rescue litters out of whatever we happened to have on-hand, including a roll of duct tape.

Related Quote

"What we do not see, what most of us never suspect of existing, is the silent but irresistible power which comes to the rescue of those who fight on in the face of discouragement." ~ **Napoleon Hill**

Robot Writer

Group Size: 4 – 10
Age Range: elementary school – adult
Intensity: Mental: easy.........♦................hard
Physical: easy........♦.................hard
Time: 10 – 20 minutes (without debrief)
Space: minimal...................♦......lots
Set Up Time: 3 minutes
Amount of Duct Tape Required: 40 - 80 feet
View Video: www.DuctTapeTeambuildingGames.com
Username: duct Password: tape

Game Objective

The team must write a word on a piece of paper using the "robot writer".

Skills Developed

Communication, Leadership, Problem Solving,

Set Up / Preparation

1. Create a "Focus Ring" device that's capable of holding a large diameter magic marker. Find the Focus Ring activity elsewhere in this book and follow the directions for constructing the Focus Ring. I recommend constructing the Focus Ring just as described in that activity and then altering it to hold the large magic marker used in this Robot Writer activity. An easy way to alter the Focus Ring to hold the magic marker is to pull the duct tape ring tight around the magic marker and then use an extra piece of duct tape to keep the ring tight around the magic marker. Refer to the photograph below.

2. Place a paper pad on the ground that the group will be writing on. During the Robot Writer game the group may accidentally overshoot the paper pad and accidentally mark on the ground (carpet, floor, etc.). If this is a problem then tape a large piece of paper on the ground (under the paper pad).

Presenting the Challenge

1. Each person in the group holds on to the end of one of the duct tape “ropes” (one rope per person). The team then pulls back gently on the ropes and position themselves equally around the center ring which holds the marker.
2. Presentation Script: “Your challenge is to write the word “TEAM” using the Robot Writer tool. You must follow all rules.” [read the rules below]

Rules

1. Each participant operates his or her own duct tape rope.
2. Participants must hold onto the end of the duct tape rope and to no other place.
3. Participants must remain at a distance of at least the length of a duct tape rope (very important).
4. The Robot Writer device may not be altered.

Safety Warning

1. The fumes of the large diameter magic marker may be unbearable for some.
2. Be aware that the group may inadvertently mark on something that shouldn’t be marked on.

Story Line

"You're a team of aliens living on different planets and you've decided it's time to collaboratively send a message to Earth. It's clear to all that the message most needed on planet Earth is that of "Teamwork". Teamwork is what the Earthlings have been lacking and it's what's holding them back. You must use your remote writing tool to send a clear message to Earth. Good luck!"

Facilitator Notes

1. I've found the best type of marker to use in this activity is a large diameter, broad tip magic marker. The large diameter makes it easier to attach to the Robot Writer device. The only thing I don't like about this kind of magic marker is the smell.
2. Participants may find themselves wrapping the duct tape rope around their hands to increase control of the Robot Writer. Encourage the group to only hold on to the end of duct tape rope.

Debriefing Suggestions

Potential questions to ask include:

- How important is one's perspective when it comes to several people working on the same project?
- What message are you communicating to the rest of the world as a team? Is it the message you want to communicate? How would you change this message?
- For Virtual Teams - - When working at a distance as a team on the same project, what strategies employed in this activity will also work on the team (in real life)?

Variations

1. Change the word the group must write. Longer words are more difficult.
2. Follow the Maze - Create a maze on a piece of paper (the kind you find in children's books) and have the group make the Robot Writer marker follow the correct pathway through the

maze. Some restaurants have children's menus or place mats with a maze - you can take this children's maze to a copy center and enlarge it for use in this activity.

3. Geometry - Have the group draw different shapes as a team. Shapes could include triangles, circles, squares, pentagon, figure 8, etc.
4. The Leader - Everyone on the team closes their eyes except one - this person is allowed to keep his eyes open for one minute. At the end of one minute he closes his eyes and someone else on the team opens his or her eyes for one minute. Keep rotating. The person whose eyes are open directs the team.
5. When I work with business teams I'll ask them to draw a complex image (logo for example). This image becomes the deliverable and I become the customer. I provide them with a short time frame to accomplish everything. At the end of this time frame, they must deliver a presentation to me.
6. Create a robot writer with long arms - this will make the activity harder.
7. To make any of these activities harder you can forbid verbal communication or require participants to use their non-dominant hand.

History

This game was taught to me by master teambuilder Jim Cain who coauthored the award winning book "Teamwork and Teamplay."
www.TeamworkAndTeamplay.com

Related Quote

"The danger of the past was that men became slaves. The danger of the future is that man may become robots." **~ Erich Fromm**

Sides Switch

Group Size: 4 – 12
Age Range: elementary school – adult
Intensity: Mental: easy.........♦................hard
Physical: easy........♦.................hard
Time: 10 – 30 minutes (without debrief)
Space: minimal..................♦......lots
Set Up Time: 5 minutes
Amount of Duct Tape Required: 20 - 30 feet
View Video: www.DuctTapeTeambuildingGames.com
Username: duct Password: tape

Game Objective

Team members switch places while standing on a long straight strip of duct tape.

Skills Developed

Communication, Problem Solving, Resource Management

Set Up / Preparation

Stick a straight strip of duct tape to the floor that is long enough for the group to comfortably stand on shoulder to shoulder.

Presenting the Challenge

1. Divide the team in half (it's nice to have an even number of players but not imperative). Have "Group A" stand to the left of center on the strip of duct tape and have "Group B" stand to the right of center on the duct tape. Ask the group to switch places. Example: start = 1 2 3 4 A B C D, end = A B C D 1 2 3 4 (where the numbers and letters represent people).
2. Presentation Script: "Your challenge is to switch places with the other small team while maintaining the order of your small team. Example: start = 1 2 3 4 A B C D, end = A B C D 1 2 3 4 (where the numbers and letters represent people)." [read the rules below]

Rules

1. When standing on the ground, a portion of your foot must be in contact with the duct tape. Violation of this rule requires a restart of the game.
2. The small team must maintain its order throughout the game.
3. The duct tape may not be altered and no other resources may be used.

Safety Warning

People may lose their balance in this activity. Remind people to simply step off the duct tape strip if they lose their balance (rather than fall out).

Story Line

"You are a group of astronauts practicing for a tricky space mission. The space station your team will be working on requires precise balancing and maneuvering. NASA has designed this challenge in an effort to mimic the actual requirements of the mission. You must be able to work together and switch places without anyone falling off the space walk."

Facilitator Notes

1. This game requires a great deal of physical contact on the part of the participants. For this reason, make sure your group is ready to work in close proximity. This may not be an appropriate activity for mixed groups (male / female).
2. This activity is (usually) simple if only four people are participating. The more people you add, the harder this activity gets.

Debriefing Suggestions

This activity requires the group to help each other a great deal in order to successfully solve this challenge (especially with fall prevention). Discuss with the group the support network they have in their home and/or work life and how it compares to the support just received in the activity. What do you like about your support network and what would you like more of?

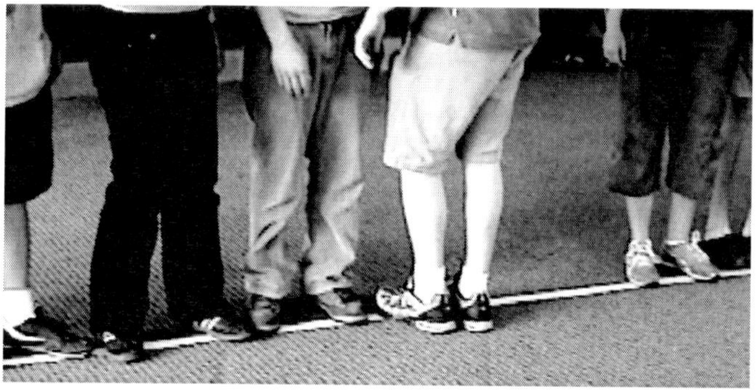

Variations

1. To significantly increase the difficulty of this game, require participants to stand on the duct tape so their feet are lined up with the duct tape (heel to toe).
2. Ask the group to stand on the duct tape strip and then ask them to line up by birth date or height or the first letter of their last name.
3. Make a giant plus sign (+) by placing a second strip of duct tape on the ground. Now you can have four smaller groups switching places all at the same time. This is hard.

History

A variation of this game called "TP Shuffle" was described in the classic teambuilding games book by Karl Rohnke **www.karlrohnke.com**

Related Quote

"Success is to be measured not so much by the position that one has reached in life... as by the obstacles which he has overcome while trying to succeed." ~ **Booker T. Washington**

Spider's Web

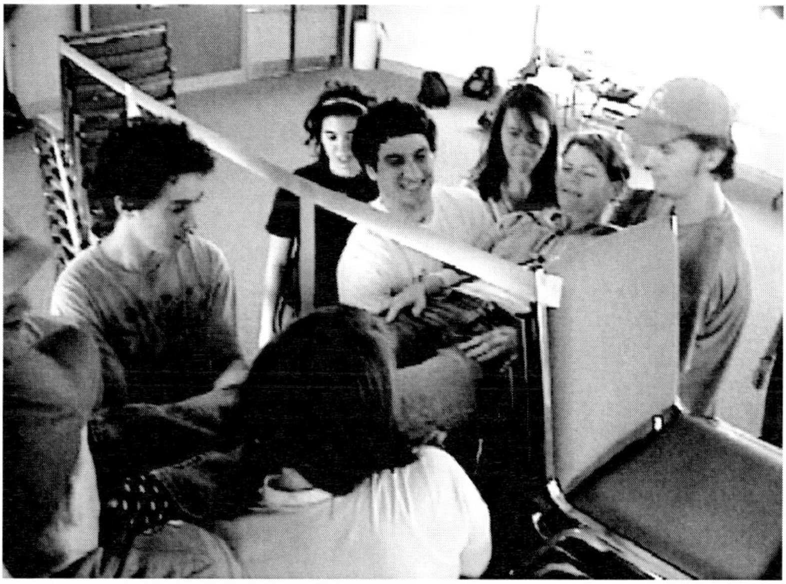

Group Size: 8 – 16
Age Range: high school – adult
Intensity: Mental: easy....................♦.....hard
Physical: easy......................♦...hard
Time: 20 – 30 minutes (without debrief)
Space: minimal...................♦......lots
Set Up Time: 15 minutes
Amount of Duct Tape Required: 40 - 50 feet
View Video: www.DuctTapeTeambuildingGames.com
Username: duct Password: tape

Game Objective

The entire group must travel through the duct tape spider's web.

Skills Developed

Trust, Planning, Leadership, Problem Solving

Set Up / Preparation

Build a spider's web:

1. When building the spider's web, your number one concern must be the safety of the participants.
2. The standard method for building a spider's web indoors is to stack chairs (that are designed to be stackable) to make two columns each measuring approximately five feet tall. If your stacked chairs are unstable don't do this activity.
3. The two columns of stacked chairs should be approximately eight feet apart.
4. Now it's time to create the actual "spider's web" by stringing the duct tape from one column of chairs to the other. The fastest and easiest stringing pattern is to create a grid, starting with the horizontal pieces of duct tape first and completing the grid by stringing the vertical pieces of duct tape last (refer to the photos). The holes should measure approximately 30 inches square. Smaller holes make the game harder. Consider creating your web with a combination of smaller and larger holes. BONUS: For those with the time and motivation, you can create a duct tape pattern between the two columns of chairs that would remind you of a real spider's web.
5. SAFETY NOTE: It's imperative to LIGHTLY attach the duct tape to the two columns of chairs. This will help prevent the chairs from falling over (and on top of people) should someone push on the duct tape. If the duct tape is lightly attached to the chairs and the duct tape is pushed, the duct tape should easily come off the chairs.
6. If you don't want to use stacks of chairs, you can create the duct tape spider's web between other things such as wide doorways, trees, columns, etc.

Presenting the Challenge

1. Ask the team to stand on one side of the spider's web.

2. Presentation Script: "Your challenge is to travel from the side of the spider's web you're now on to the other side. You must obey the following rules throughout the game." [read the rules below]

Rules

1. Team members must travel THROUGH the spider's web. You can't travel over, under or around it.
2. Participants may not alter the spider's web.
3. No member of the team may touch the spider's web (duct tape) at any time no matter what side of the spider's web he or she is on.
4. Should a touch occur, offer the group a penalty or a combination of the following penalties:
    - The person who touched must go back.
    - The entire team starts over again.
    - Pass 2 people who are connected together through the web.
    - Allow the group to decide on an appropriate penalty.
5. Once an individual successfully makes it through a hole, that hole is closed (see "Variations" below).

6. Participants may not jump or dive through web openings. Anyone traveling through the web must be spotted.
7. Only the supplied equipment may be used. NOTE: Do not supply the group with any additional equipment. This rule will keep the group from using boards or other devices to help them travel through the web openings.

Safety Warning

1. Because lifting is involved, this is considered an advanced game. If the group does not posses the physical strength or the appropriate level of leadership skills, do not attempt this game.
2. If you (the facilitator) ever feel that the group is operating in an unsafe manner you must immediately stop the game.
3. Follow the safety procedures for spotting described at the beginning of this book.
4. People with knee, shoulder or back injuries should not participate.
5. If possible, place a pad (gymnastics mat) on the ground underneath the spider's web. This will provide a cushion should someone fall to the ground during this game.

Story Line

"Your team is traveling through the Amazon jungle and the path you must take has a giant spider's web across it. There is no way around this so you must travel through the spider's web. Don't touch the spider's web or the giant spider will wake up and chase you!"

Facilitator Notes

1. Due to the fact that lifting and spotting is involved, I consider this an advanced teambuilding game. Not all teams are ready for this activity.
2. During this game you (the facilitator) will be right in there with the group spotting them. You need to encourage everyone else to be safe during the game as well.

3. Some groups may want to practice passing people through the web prior to the actual game. Allowing the group to practice on the web itself can take away some of the unknown aspects of the activity. If you do decide to let the group practice, consider setting some limitations on the practice (time, number of tries, etc.). Practice can always be held in another area with the group imagining the actual spider's web.

Debriefing Suggestions

Because this activity requires team members to help each other pass through openings, it lends itself to debriefing questions such as:

- In this game, the openings were made of duct tape. What "openings" exist for us as a team right now that we aren't utilizing fully? What openings would we like to create?
- This game required a balance of planning and doing. What is true about how our team balanced these two during the game that is also true about how we balance the two in real life? Are there important lessons about the balance between planning and doing that we must understand to move forward as a team?
- When being passed through the web you were forced to trust your teammates to take care of you. What noticeable and measurable changes would happen on our team if we trusted each other 10 times more?

Variations

1. Normally a hole is closed and made unusable after someone passes through that hole. You may need to re-open a hole under certain conditions. For example, if you have only 10 holes but have 15 people you will need to allow the group to use 5 of the holes twice. In this scenario you can let the team decide which holes will be used twice or you (the facilitator) can decide it and tell them.
2. Divide the team in half. Have one group start on one side of the spider's web and the other group start on the other side of it. The goal is for the two groups to switch sides. The same rules for use of the holes apply in this variation. Hopefully the two groups will choose to cooperate.

History

This game was first described in Karl Rohnke's classic teambuilding games book "Cowstails and Cobras II" **www.karlrohnke.com**

Related Quote

"The bird a nest, the spider a web, man friendship."

~ William Blake

Stopwatch

Group Size: 6 – 15
Age Range: elementary school – adult
Intensity: Mental: easy.........♦................hard
Physical: easy..................♦......hard
Time: 5 – 10 minutes (without debrief)
Space: minimal..................♦......lots
Set Up Time: 5 minutes
Amount of Duct Tape Required: 40 - 50 feet
View Video: www.DuctTapeTeambuildingGames.com
Username: duct Password: tape

Game Objective

Turn the circle of duct tape around 360 degrees as quickly as possible.

Skills Developed

Fun, Energizer, Process Improvement, Goals

Set Up / Preparation

1. Create a 15-feet long section of duct tape "rope". It takes three people to create this duct tape rope: one person who dispenses duct tape and two people to hold the ends of the duct tape. Pull off a 15-feet section of duct tape and have two volunteers hold the ends of this piece of duct tape. Repeat this process three more times, allowing all four long pieces of duct tape to stick to each other. Now have the duct tape holders twist the duct tape rope (the four "strands") - this will help bind the four 15-feet long strips of duct tape together to make one duct tape rope. If you can, try to string out the 15-feet long strips of duct tape so that the sticky sides are not exposed (this isn't critical). NOTE: This is the same duct tape rope that is used in the games Balance Tug, Turnstile, Throw Up, and Yurt Circle.
2. Make a circle out of the duct tape rope. Overlap the ends of the duct tape rope by 12 inches to form a circle. Using a separate piece of duct tape, tightly wrap the overlapped area so the overlapped area is secure. It's important to do a good job taping the ends together to form a circle because the group will be pulling on the circle in this game and it would be unsafe for the circle to come apart.
3. Mark the duct tape circle. During the game, the team will have to rotate the duct tape circle 360 degrees. Mark one point on the circle by hanging (taping) a 12 - 18 inch long strip of duct tape.
4. Using two pieces of duct tape (each measuring approximately 12 inches) create the letter "V" on the ground. The point of this V will designate the start-stop line (point) during the game.

Presenting the Challenge

1. Have the group surround the duct tape circle (ring) and hold onto it with only the right hand (forming a circle). Make sure each person holds on tightly.

2. Have the group rotate the duct tape circle (by walking in a circle) so the strip of duct tape hanging off the duct tape circle matches up with the point on the giant letter V on the ground.
3. While holding onto the duct tape circle with their right hand, the group must now kneel down (on one knee) while facing a clockwise direction.
4. The facilitator will use a stopwatch to time the group as they run around in a circle to move the duct tape marker hanging from the duct tape circle.
5. Presentation Script: "Your challenge is to hold onto the duct tape circle with your right hand and run around, causing the duct tape circle to rotate a full 360 and do this as fast as you can." [read the rules below]

Rules

1. The stopwatch starts when the facilitator yells GO!
2. You must start and stop from the "ready position" which is: right hand on the duct tape rope, one knee on the ground, and the marker on the duct tape circle is over the top of the point of the giant letter V on the ground.
3. If anyone releases the duct tape rope the attempt is nullified.

Safety Warning

1. It is important to select a location for this game that has a playing surface that is conducive to fast movement. If you play indoors, make sure the ground is clean (not slippery). If you play outdoors it is best to select a flat grassy area.
2. Groups that run around too fast may have team members who lose their footing and fall down. If this happens suspend the game and help the group find a way to complete this activity safely.
3. If the group is being reckless stop the game.

Story Line

"Your team has entered a big sailboat race. When the signal is given, all sailboats will quickly raise their anchor by turning a giant ring. History has proven that the team who raises anchor first inevitably wins the race. So when you hear the signal, turn your giant ring as fast as you can to raise your anchor! Good luck!"

Facilitator Notes

This is a fun, high energy game that requires strong teamwork to do well.

Debriefing Suggestions

Potential questions to pose to the group might be:

Describe a situation in the past when your team used time wisely / effectively?

Do you ever waste time? Why?

How do you like to spend your free time?

Does time move fast or does time move slowly?

Variations

1. After the first attempt, give the group another try to lower their score and set a new "world record".

2. Have the group make the duct tape circle rotate first in a clockwise direction then immediately back in a counterclockwise direction – this creates a back and forth look to the game.

History

This game was taught to me by an intern when I worked for the YMCA.

Related Quote

"It is impossible to travel faster than the speed of light, and certainly not desirable, as one's hat keeps blowing off."

~ Woody Allen

Swiss Cheese Challenge

Group Size: 4 – 8

Age Range: elementary school – adult

Intensity: <u>Mental</u>: easy....♦.....................hard

<u>Physical</u>: easy....♦.....................hard

Time: 10 – 15 minutes (without debrief)

Space: minimal....♦.....................lots

Set Up Time: 30 minutes

Amount of Duct Tape Required: approximately 25 feet

View Video: www.DuctTapeTeambuildingGames.com

Username: duct Password: tape

Game Objective

Make the ball travel around the holes without falling through a hole or off the duct tape square.

Skills Developed

Communication, Problem Solving, Planning

Set Up / Preparation

1. CREATE THE SQUARE: Using duct tape, create a square piece of "fabric" measuring 16 inches x 16 inches. Start by tearing off multiple 16 inch strips of duct tape then laying them next to each other (parallel to each other) - sticky side up - and overlapping the edges slightly so they stick to each other. Once you've laid enough pieces next to each other to create a square start laying 16 inch long pieces of duct tape perpendicular to the original pieces (sticky sides together). Eventually you'll end up with a square piece of duct tape "fabric" with the grey (non-sticky) side showing on both sides of the square.
2. CUT HOLES: Cut a 1 1/4 inch diameter hole in the center of the square piece of duct tape "fabric". Cut 1 1/4 inch holes between the center hole and the four corners making a total of 5 holes.
3. MAKE A BALL: Using duct tape, create a small ball (the size of a marble). Cut or tear off a four inch long strip of duct tape and then rip it in half lengthwise and rip those pieces in half lengthwise (total of 4 pieces). Carefully roll up one of these narrow four inch long strips of duct tape into the shape of a tiny ball. Take the next four inch long narrow strip of duct tape and continue adding to the ball. Repeat the process until the ball is about the size of a marble. The tighter (more compact) and smoother you make the ball the better (it will roll better).

Presenting the Challenge

1. Have the team of 4 to 8 people stand up and surround the "Swiss cheese" square (piece of duct tape "fabric"). The team members space themselves out evenly around the Swiss cheese and grab hold of the edge with two hands to create a table-top effect.
2. <u>Presentation Script:</u> "Your challenge is to make this duct tape ball roll around each of the five holes (individually, not collectively) without the ball falling through a hole or off the Swiss cheese fabric." [read the rules below]

Rules

1. If the ball falls off the Swiss cheese or through a hole, the game starts over.
2. Participants must hold onto the Swiss cheese with both hands throughout the activity and only on the edge.
3. The Swiss cheese must be stretched out so that it remains flat (like a table top).
4. The Swiss cheese must be held so that it remains at its maximum size (the Swiss cheese may not be "gathered up" around the edges to change its shape or size).
5. The group must hold the swiss cheese in the air (i.e. not laid on the ground or on any other surface).
6. If the ball starts to roll off the Swiss cheese, participants can use their body like a "bumper" to keep the ball on the Swiss cheese (hands may not let go of the Swiss cheese though).
7. Swiss cheese holes may not be blocked. Should a ball fall through a hole, it may not be knocked back through the hole (example: kicking ball with foot back through the hole).
8. The Swiss cheese (duct tape fabric) may not be altered.

Safety Warning

The small duct tape balls are choking hazards. Keep them away from small children.

Story Line

"You are a team of secret agent spies faced with unlocking a safe containing the codes to the manufacturing plans for a duct tape blimp. If you get the plans you can float to safety. To unlock the safe you must work cooperatively to move a small ball around a series of holes on a duct tape square. Be careful. Danger lurks at every turn."

Facilitator Notes

1. It is common for a group to start off without a plan of action (example: "Lets do this hole first, then that hole"). Frustration

can set in as the ball rolls through a hole or off the top multiple times. Success is usually achieved when the group decides on which hole to go after and they do so in a calm and deliberate fashion.

2. If you have a group larger than 8 people just make multiple "Swiss cheese" squares so multiple groups can play at the same time.

Debriefing Suggestions

This activity lends itself well to discussions about achieving success despite the obstacles in our lives. Lifelong success is rarely achieved through chance – instead, the successful make a plan, continually evaluate, and then change the plan as needed. When everyone on the team is committed to the plan success is much more likely.

- What strategies did you apply here to experience success and are any of these strategies applicable in real life situations?
- How is this activity just like real life? How is it unlike real life?

Variations

1. Provide the group with a time limitation (example: only 10 minutes to complete this activity).
2. Require the group to complete the activity without verbal communication.
3. To make this easier, cover some of the holes with a piece of duct tape (fewer holes = easier). As the group improves, uncover more holes.
4. Require the group to circle the holes in a specific order (hole 1, then hole 3, then hole 5, etc.).
5. Start the group off with only one ball and then have them graduate to completing the same task with 2 or even 3 balls simultaneously.
6. Try cutting holes of different sizes (diameters).
7. Here is a more involved version. Have the group identify the top 5 things that hold them back in some way. Then have

them write these top 5 on the “Swiss cheese” square (next to a hole). Now ask the group to complete the basic challenge (described above). To debrief this exercise, ask the group to find strategies that promoted success on the Swiss cheese square (i.e. how to avoid the top 5 pitfalls) and identify which of these strategies can be translated to avoiding the same pitfalls in real life.

History

I developed this game in 2001 and it appears in Volume 2 of my multimedia teambuilding games training CDs. The original design uses a 5 feet x 8 feet poly tarp with 6 inch diameter holes and a tennis ball. Learn more about my best selling multimedia training CDs at **www.TeachMeTeamwork.com**

Related Quote

“Swiss Cheese is a rip-off! It's the only cheese I can bite into and miss!” ~ **Mitch Hedberg**

Tail Tag

Group Size: 10 – 50
Age Range: elementary school – adult
Intensity: Mental: easy.. ♦........................hard
Physical: easy........♦.................hard
Time: 5 – 15 minutes (without debrief)
Space: minimal..................♦......lots
Set Up Time: 5 minutes
Amount of Duct Tape Required: 20 - 50 feet
View Video: www.DuctTapeTeambuildingGames.com
Username: duct Password: tape

Game Objective

Be the last one to have your duct tape tail removed from your belt line.

Skills Developed

Fun, Energizer

Set Up / Preparation

1. Create one duct tape "tail" for each participant. To make one tail, pull off two strips of duct tape measuring approximately 18 inches each. Carefully stick the two pieces together (sticky sides together) to make one tail measuring 18 inches long.
2. Create your boundary / play area by placing duct tape on the ground for boundary markers. The smaller you make it the faster the game goes. A larger area makes the game last longer.

Presenting the Challenge

1. Supply each person with a duct tape tail and ask them to place the end (1/3) of it in their waste band, allowing the majority of it (at least 2/3) to hang out like a tail. Hang the tail on the side or the back.
2. Ask everyone to stand at the perimeter of the playing area and at an equal distance from other players.
3. <u>Presentation Script:</u> "In a moment, but not yet, I'll yell "GO!" and when I do you'll do two things: (1) pull other people's tails from their waist bands and (2) try not to have your own tail pulled from your waist band." [read the rules below]

Rules

1. You can move around anywhere inside the playing area.
2. You aren't allowed to guard your tail or otherwise use your hands to keep people from grabbing your tail. Turning and twisting your body is allowed (so is running).
3. If your tail gets pulled away then you must immediately stop and place your tail on the ground and then place one foot on it. You can still keep playing – trying to pull other people's tails away – but you must keep one foot on your tail at all times

(you can pivot in circles) and the tail must remain in the same location.

Safety Warning

Some people (some groups) will want to move too fast during this game and that will cause an unsafe playing situation. It's possible for people to have head-on collisions in this game if they aren't being careful. Be prepared to stop action.

Story Line

"On the planet of Ductapicus everyone has a tail that is removable. If you were to travel to Ductapicus you would need to be able to play this game because their culture values having fun, quickness and teamwork. So let's play!"

Facilitator Notes

During the game you might find some players cheating by blocking others from grabbing their tail. For some, it's hard to have fun unless they're winning (even if they have to cheat to win). When I see this type of behavior I usually don't make a big fuss about it. I try to keep it light and fun. I will remind players before a new round that blocking (with hands or arms) is illegal.

This game won't work well unless the group is ready for a game with lots of fast, quick movement.

Debriefing Suggestions

When I lead this game I usually don't debrief or process it (I just play for fun). It is possible to use this activity to discuss issues such as working on your own vs. working as a team.

Variations

The activity becomes much more difficult if you allow people to put more than half of the tail inside their pants / belt loop. And if you make the playing area really large (like the size of a basketball court) the game will become super hard and take a long time to play.

History

This game was taught to me by a group of children.

Related Quote

"It gets you nowhere if the other person's tail is only just in sight for the second half of the conversation." ***~ Winnie the Pooh***

Team Skis

Group Size: 2 – 10

Age Range: middle school – adult

Intensity: Mental: easy.........♦................hard

Physical: easy................♦.........hard

Time: 5 – 15 minutes (without debrief)

Space: minimal.................. ♦......lots

Set Up Time: 5 minutes

Amount of Duct Tape Required: 8 - 20 feet

View Video: www.DuctTapeTeambuildingGames.com

Username: duct Password: tape

Game Objective

With everyone's feet stuck to long strips of duct tape, the team travels as a unit from Point A to Point B.

Skills Developed

Clear Communication, Leadership, Trust, Planning

Set Up / Preparation

Create two parallel lines (each 10 feet long) on the ground using duct tape. The lines should be 20 - 30 feet apart.

Presenting the Challenge

1. Ask the group to stand behind one of the parallel lines and face the second parallel line.
2. Have everyone find a partner. If you have an odd number of people then there will be one group of 3 people.
3. Provide each pair with two strips of duct tape that are long enough for this team of two to put their feet on (lengthwise). Lay the duct tape on the ground parallel to each other (approximately 6 inches apart) STICKY SIDE UP.
4. Have each pair line up - one person behind the other, both facing the same direction. Then this team of two carefully steps on the duct tape and thus, the tape sticks to their shoes and connects the pair.
5. NOTE: Participants MUST wear shoes (no sandals).
6. <u>Presentation Script:</u> "Your challenge is to travel from the line you're now behind (the starting position) over to and across the other (parallel) line. You must follow and obey the rules throughout the game." [read the rules below]

Rules

1. Feet must remain stuck to the duct tape from tip of shoe to heel.
2. No ripping of the duct tape.
3. Violation of a rule may result in a penalty. Sample penalties include: *can't verbally communicate for 2 minutes, must turn around and face backwards, must close eyes for 2 minutes, whenever you want to communicate verbally you must sing like an opera singer, whenever you talk you must speak*

backwards, the entire group starts all over, the entire group does 5 pushups, etc.

Safety Warning

1. People with knee, ankle or back injuries should not participate.
2. Everyone must wear shoes during this activity (no sandals). Do not put duct tape on skin.
3. Watch out for the "domino effect" – this happens when one person begins to fall into another person causing the entire group to fall.
4. Encourage the group to act safely and warn them of the domino effect.
5. Always spot the group to prevent injuries.

Story Line

"While traveling through the Amazon jungle in search of a cure for cancer, your team has come across a mysterious 60 foot wide river filled with crocodiles. Luckily, your guide has brought along two strips of magical duct tape which will allow your team to cross over the river without sinking. If the duct tape tears then the magic disappears (you sink)."

Facilitator Notes

1. Use high quality duct tape (thick and strong) for this game. Cheap duct tape (thin and weak) will tear too easily.
2. TYPICAL SOLUTION – The team picks a leader who then encourages everyone to lift their right feet simultaneously. The group then repeats this action with their left feet. The group usually yells some type of chant together such as "1 – 2 – 3 RIGHT, 1 – 2 – 3 LEFT!"
3. This challenge is unique in that it's easy to figure out <u>how</u> to do but difficult to actually pull off. This challenge gets harder as the group gets larger (more people require a greater degree of concentration, balance, communication, etc.). This activity necessitates the exact timing of the group's efforts for success and should, therefore, be used with a group that has worked successfully in the past (and now needs a harder challenge).

Debriefing Suggestions

Once, when working with a team on goal setting and goal achieving, I had the group list out their team goals on a large piece of paper and then tape it to a wall. I then asked the group to identify the obstacles that stood in their path to achieving these team goals. I asked the group to move to the opposite side of the room (opposite from their goal sheet) and then provided the group with a set of duct tape Team Skis and told them they must reach their goals - this would be metaphorically represented by the group traveling across the room on the duct tape Team Skis. I then placed a number of obstacles in their way that the group was not allowed to move. The physical obstacles represented the "real life" obstacles. Obstacles included: chairs, desk, mousetraps, and a string 4 feet off the ground they had to travel under (and not touch). When the group was done, I asked them to identify the top three team skills that helped them make it to their goal sheet.

Variations

1. Have the large group (team) first work in pairs, then in teams of 4 and then in larger and larger groups. The larger the group working together the harder it is to play.
2. Have every other person face backwards.
3. Have the group travel to a spot 20 yards away and then return to the start line moving in reverse.
4. Require the group to move *sideways* from one point to another.
5. Create a race situation between two teams. You can allow the teams to practice for 10 minutes before you start. If the teams practice within sight of each other they will end up borrowing ideas from each other. If you separate them completely (sight and sound) the groups will have to come up with ideas on their own.
6. Provide obstacles for the team to travel around, through, or under (cones, doorways, tables, etc.).
7. Provide 3 strips of duct tape for two groups of people to work collaboratively. Line up the 3 strips of duct tape in 3 parallel lines and then have the two groups stand on the strips of duct tape like normal with the twist that the two teams must share the "middle" strip of duct tape. The two groups must travel as one. This is accomplished by having the two teams shift their weight to the shared (middle) strip of duct tape while simultaneously lifting and moving the outside strips of duct tape. They would then all shift their weight to their outside legs as they lift and move their inside legs forward (remember that their inside legs share a common strip of duct tape).
8. Have two groups, each with their own set of duct tape Team Skis. The two groups must pick up a bucket filled with water ("nuclear waste") and transport it to a "safe" spot. The two groups must stay at least 10 yards apart from each other and

must stay at least 5 yards away from the bucket. Supply the groups with one section of rope that has a hook attached to the middle of it. The hook will allow the group to hook onto the bucket handle. If any water is spilled provide the group with a penalty (example: start over).

History

This duct tape Team Skis game is a variation on a game called "Trolleys" described in the classic teambuilding games book "Silver Bullets" by Karl Rohnke **www.karlrohnke.com**

Related Quote

"Skiing: I do not participate in any sport with ambulances at the bottom of the hill" ~ **Erma Bombeck**

Throw Up

Group Size: 3 – 5
Age Range: middle school – adult
Intensity: Mental: easy....♦.....................hard
Physical: easy....♦.....................hard
Time: 5 – 10 minutes (without debrief)
Space: minimal..........♦.............lots
Set Up Time: 5 minutes
Amount of Duct Tape Required: 40 - 50 feet
View Video: www.DuctTapeTeambuildingGames.com
Username: duct Password: tape

Game Objective

As a small team, throw the duct tape circle into the air and then quickly reposition yourselves so the circle lands on the perimeter of the team (on the ground).

Skills Developed

Problem Solving, Planning, Leadership

Set Up / Preparation

1. Create a 15-feet long section of duct tape "rope". It takes three people to create this duct tape rope: one person who dispenses duct tape and two people to hold the ends of the duct tape. Pull off a 15-feet section of duct tape and have two volunteers hold the ends of this piece of duct tape. Repeat this process three more times, allowing all four long pieces of duct tape to stick to each other. Now have the duct tape holders twist the duct tape rope (the four "strands"). This will help bind the four 15-feet long strips of duct tape together to make one duct tape rope. If you can, try to string out the 15-feet long strips of duct tape so that their sticky sides are not exposed (this isn't critical). NOTE: This is the same duct tape rope that is used in the games Balance Tug, Turnstile, Stopwatch, and Yurt Circle.
2. Make a circle out of the duct tape rope. Overlap the ends of the duct tape rope by 12 inches to form a circle. Using a separate piece of duct tape, tightly wrap the overlapped area to make the overlapped area secure. It's important to do a good job taping the ends together to form a circle because the group may pull on the circle in this game and it would be unsafe for the circle to come apart.
3. If you have a large group you'll start by creating small teams of 3 people. Each small team will need their own duct tape circle.

Presenting the Challenge

1. Get into small teams of 3 people. Provide each small team with a duct tape circle.
2. Presentation Script: "Your challenge is to toss your duct tape circle in the air and then quickly reposition yourselves in such a way that the circle lands on the ground around your team (encircles your team)." [read the rules below]

Rules

Should the duct tape circle land on you and get stuck after you've thrown it in the air you may not manipulate the circle or otherwise manually make it fall to the ground.

Safety Warning

Some teams will be overzealous in their desire to quickly move to form a small group after throwing the duct tape circle in the air and this can result in people getting hurt (example: bumping heads). Warn the team in advance about this problem.

Story Line

"While traveling through the Amazon jungle your team has encountered an unusual giant snake. To keep the snake from following you and eating all your duct tape, you must throw it in the air in such a way that it lands in a circle around your team. This will cause the snake to enter a deep sleep which will prevent the snake from following you."

Facilitator Notes

This activity is relatively easy for a group of three people but adding even one more person (group of four) makes it much more difficult.

Because participants come rushing towards each other face first (chest first) and then collide (hopefully gently) this activity may not be appropriate for some groups.

Debriefing Suggestions

On a scale of 1 to 10, how close are we as a team? Explain your response.

What would bring us closer together?

What keeps us apart?

Variations

After the group has success with three people, add a fourth person (groups of four). Then make groups of five.

History

I was taught this game by Jim Cain who authored the award winning teambuilding games book “Teamwork & Teamplay”. **www.teamworkandteamplay.com**

Related Quote

“Until he extends his circle of compassion to include all living things, man will not himself find peace.” **~ Albert Schweitzer**

Touch the Roll

Group Size: 8 – 20
Age Range: elementary school – adult
Intensity: Mental: easy...♦......................hard
Physical: easy......♦...................hard
Time: 5 – 15 minutes (without debrief)
Space: minimal.......♦..................lots
Set Up Time: 1 minute
Amount of Duct Tape Required: one roll (pulling tape off not required)
View Video: www.DuctTapeTeambuildingGames.com
Username: duct Password: tape

Game Objective

Everyone must touch the roll of duct tape at the same time.

Skills Developed

Fun, Problem Solving, Process Improvement, Resource Management

Set Up / Preparation

Get one roll of duct tape and the group together.

Presenting the Challenge

1. Gather the group together and then read the script below.
2. Presentation Script: "Your challenge is for everyone on the team to touch this roll of duct tape at the same time." [read the rules below]

Rules

1. No touching anyone else during the game. If anyone is touching anyone else (includes hair and clothing) the facilitator will notify the group and the group must continue trying to find a way for everyone to touch the roll of duct tape without touching each other.
2. The roll of duct tape may not be changed from the way it is presented.

Safety Warning

Some people may find themselves needing to become a contortionist to complete this activity. If you (the facilitator) see someone getting into a position that is potentially harmful you must stop the game.

Story Line

"The roll of duct tape will give off positive, sticky energy to the team that is able to touch the roll at the same time but not touch each other. Since we're all in need of positive, sticky energy, let's all touch this roll of duct tape!"

Facilitator Notes

1. This is a great group problem solving activity to do at the beginning of a program. I like this because it requires people to be close physically yet prohibits touching. This activity begins the investment required to ease barriers around touching and close proximity which is particularly useful if you plan to lead activities like All Aboard, Caterpillar Traverse, or Team Skis.
2. This is a great activity to lead with large groups (200+). See below.

Debriefing Suggestions

Because the group must come together and focus their collective attention on one item (the roll of duct tape) this game lends itself to debrief questions like:

- If we were to focus our attention on one aspect of our business what would it be? How would our focus change or influence our actions?
- On a scale of 1 - 10 (with 10 being the highest / best), how would you rate our closeness as a team? What would help us become closer as a team? What keeps us apart?

Variations

1. After the group has successfully completed the basic challenge outlined above, require the group to follow the same rules AND add these rules: one person in the group must touch with his or her nose, another with the elbow, another with the knee, and another with the tip of the shoe (which must stay on their foot) AND then give the group 2 minutes to solve this.
2. To lead this activity with a large group (20 – 200+), start off by supplying the group with lots of rolls of duct tape (about 1 roll per 10 people). Tell the group that everyone must be touching a roll at the end of 30 seconds (and you can't be touching anyone/anything else). No need to divide the group up, just pass the rolls out, give the directions and start counting. People will scurry around trying to find a place to fit in. Once everyone has succeeded (this is easy with so many rolls), tell

the group there has been a "reduction in funding" and they will have to "produce the same results" (all touching) even though there are fewer resources (fewer rolls). This gives you the reason to take a couple of the rolls away. Now give the group 30 seconds to find a spot and touch a roll. Once they succeed, repeat the process (take more rolls away). If someone violates the "don't touch anyone/anything else" rule I usually serve him or her a penalty – something like singing one round of row-row-row your boat while hopping around the room. Once the penalty is served they will be permitted to join back in.

History

This game was taught to me by master teambuilder Betsy Hipple.

Related Quote

"When you stop putting yourself on the line, and you don't touch your own heart, how do you expect to touch other people?"

~ Tori Amos

Traffic Jam

Group Size: 6 – 10
Age Range: middle school – adult
Intensity: <u>Mental</u>: easy....................♦.....hard
<u>Physical</u>: easy....♦.....................hard
Time: 15 – 45 minutes (without debrief)
Space: minimal......♦...................lots
Set Up Time: 5 minutes
Amount of Duct Tape Required: 10 - 15 feet
View Video: www.DuctTapeTeambuildingGames.com
Username: duct   Password: tape

Game Objective

Solve this human size puzzle. Half of the group travels in one direction while the other half travels in the opposite direction along stepping stones.

Skills Developed

Communication, Problem Solving, Creativity

Set Up / Preparation

This game can be played by groups of 6 to 10 people. However, for the sake of the description of this game, I assume you will have 8 people playing this game.

Create The Playing Area: Using duct tape, create 9 "squares" (spaces) on the ground that the 8 players will utilize during the game. The squares can be made in different ways:

a. The fastest and easiest way to create the 9 squares is to simply tear off 9 short pieces of duct tape (2 to 3 inches in length) and stick them on the ground (spacing them out) in the shape of the letter "L". There will be four pieces of duct tape on either side of the corner piece. The distance between each piece of duct tape will be approximately two feet. During the game, players will either stand on top of the duct tape pieces or behind them.

b. An alternate way to create 9 squares is to create 9 index card sized "spots" out of duct tape. These spots can be used over and over because you'll be creating the spots in such a way that no sticky side is exposed. During the game, players will either stand on top of the duct tape spots or behind them.

c. The most elaborate way to create 9 squares (spaces) is to make 9 squares on the ground out of duct tape. The squares will measure 2 feet x 2 feet. During the game, players will stand inside the squares.

I recommend labeling each square (space) with a letter (A - I). This will make it easier to describe the game and the rules.

Presenting the Challenge

1. Eight team members (players) are to stand in the following squares, one in each square: A, B, C, D, F, G, H and I. Square "E" is to remain empty at the beginning of the game.
2. <u>Presentation Script:</u> "Your challenge is for team members 1, 2, 3, and 4 to move to squares F, G, H, and I respectively AND

team members 5, 6, 7, and 8 to move to squares A, B, C, and D respectively. Refer to the diagram." [read the rules below]

Rules

1. Players must stand on/in a square unless they are moving.
2. Only one player may move at a time
3. Players may only move forward (towards the direction the player must end in).
4. Only one player on a square at a time.
5. Players may use the corner square (position "E").
6. Players may only "jump" a maximum of one person at a time.
7. The playing area may not be altered.
8. Violation of a rule may result in a penalty. Penalties might include no verbal communication for 1 minute for the one person or the entire group, blindfolding one person for 5 minutes or for the rest of the activity, who ever talks must do so while clapping their hands repeatedly, etc.

Start

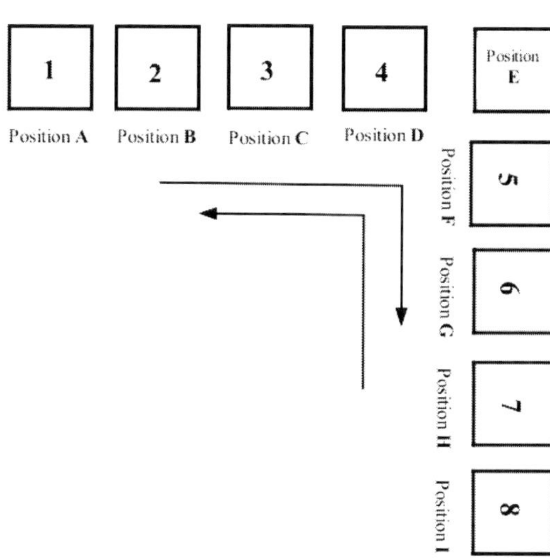

Finish

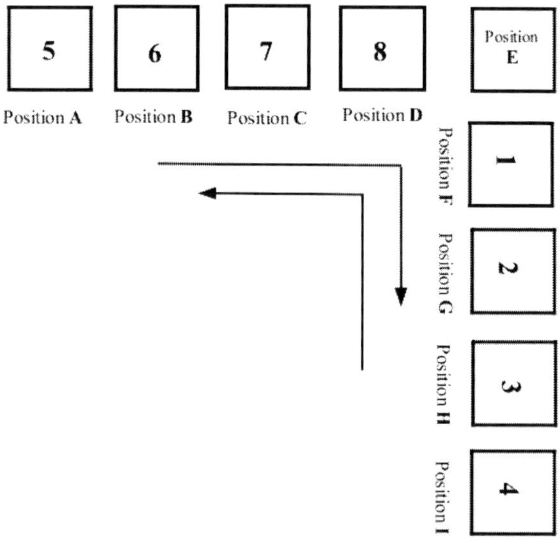

Safety Warning

I consider this activity to be relatively safe unless you release wild dogs into the playing area (not advised).

Story Line

"Your team has entered the World Champion Team Duct Tape Puzzle Solving Contest and is now faced with your ultimate challenge. Can you solve the problem you've been given to win the world championship?"

Facilitator Notes

This activity requires lots of communication, problem solving skills and patience from the group. You might see a group where each person is totally engaged and other groups where two or three individuals are doing all the work while the others are along for the ride. This is definitely a more cerebral activity.

Debriefing Suggestions

I like to use this activity when a group needs to discuss or work on the creation of specific reproducible plans to achieve success. When I lead this activity I'll require a group to create a solution sheet that spells out each and every step they've taken. The solution represents a precise step-by-step approach that (nearly) any group could follow to solve the Traffic Jam activity. I'll then ask the group what skills were required to create such a document and I'll ask what value the document holds. I'll then ask the group to make the metaphorical jump to "real life" - in other words, what specific skills are transferable to creating a similar step-by-step success plan for their current (real life) situation?

Variations

1. Require the group to repeat the solution on demand. You can also offer the group "bonus points" if they finish the solution in less than the given amount of time.
2. To simplify this activity, give the group only 7 spaces to start with (instead of 9). In this situation, you would only have 6 people playing the game. The directions are virtually the same.
3. This game requires you to have an even number of players. If you have an odd number of people in the group (example: 7) then add an item to represent a person (example: chair) and the group has to manually move that chair throughout the game.

History

A description of this game first appeared in Karl Rohnke's classic book of teambuilding games entield "Silver Bullets". **www.karlrohnke.com**

Related Quote

"Natives who beat drums to drive off evil spirits are objects of scorn to smart Americans who blow horns to break up traffic jams." ~ **Mary Ellen Kelly**

Solution to Traffic Jam

(see the grid below)

1. In the following solution there are a total of 24 moves.
2. The 8 participants maintain the same number throughout the activity.
3. The spaces (spots that participants step on) are identified with the letters A through I (the first 9 letters of the alphabet). The spaces do not move or change - only the participants move (from space to space).
4. There could be more than one solution but this is the only one I know of.

Move Number	Person Number	Moves to Space
1	4	E
2	5	D
3	6	F
4	4	G
5	3	E
6	2	C
7	5	B
8	6	D
9	7	F
10	8	H
11	4	I
12	3	G

13	2	E
14	1	C
15	5	A
16	6	B
17	7	D
18	8	F
19	3	H
20	2	G
21	1	E
22	7	C
23	8	D
24	1	F

Trust V

Group Size: 4 – 20
Age Range: middle school – adult
Intensity: Mental: easy.........♦................hard
Physical: easy....................♦.....hard
Time: 10 – 30 minutes (without debrief)
Space: minimal...................♦......lots
Set Up Time: 2 minutes
Amount of Duct Tape Required: 20 - 30 feet
View Video: www.DuctTapeTeambuildingGames.com
Username: duct Password: tape

Game Objective

Working with a partner, travel from one end of the giant letter "V" to the other.

Skills Developed

Trust, Communication, Roles and Responsibilities, Planning, Goals

Set Up / Preparation

1. Create a giant letter “V” on the ground. The sides of the V measure approximately 12 - 15 feet. The opening of the V (ends of the letter V) should measure 6 - 8 feet (wider = harder).
2. When creating the giant letter V on the ground, select a surface that is clean and covered in carpet that is not slippery. Participants must wear shoes that have good grip on the carpet. The carpeted surface provides a safer surface to land on should someone fall down.

Presenting the Challenge

1. IMPORTANT: Read the section at the beginning of this book on “Safety” and “The Importance of Spotting.” If your group or any member of your group isn’t ready for this activity don’t do it.
2. Talk with your group about how this activity is a trust building exercise and this is the time for everyone to focus in and exhibit the kind of behavior that builds trust. This helps set the correct tone for this activity.
3. Ask the participants to partner up with someone who is about the same height and weight.
4. Find two volunteers who are ready to be the first to attempt the Trust V and then find two other people who are willing to act as spotters. You (the facilitator) will then teach everyone how to properly act as spotters when there are participants on the Trust V and you can do this effectively through demonstration.
5. Spotters are very important in this game. If they don’t do their job properly someone might get hurt. Spotters will maneuver under the participants’ arms when there is enough space between the participants. The participants must move slowly down the Trust V and the spotters will carefully move with the participants.

6. Spotters will bend over and brace their arms on their knees. Refer to the photo.
7. Presentation Script: "Your challenge is to travel as a team of two from one end of this Trust V to the other. Before starting on this challenge, your team of two must know who your spotters will be. As you travel down the Trust V you'll need to lean on each other. Interlocking fingers is not permitted. The further you travel down the Trust V the harder the activity becomes. If you sense you might fall or loose your footing then simply step forward or lean on your spotters. Your goal is to travel as a team to the end of the Trust V." [read the rules below]

Rules

1. Before traveling down the Trust V with your partner you must secure your two spotters.
2. Spotters must move into position when there is room between the participants.
3. When traveling down the Trust V with your partner your feet must not cross the duct tape line (crossing to inside the V). Your feet can touch the duct tape but not cross it.
4. For safety reasons, interlocking of fingers between partners is prohibited.
5. If one or both participants steps into (or falls into) the Trust V (area inside the V) the team must start over.

Safety Warning

1. Before leading this game, read the section on "Safety" and "The Importance of Spotting" at the beginning of this book.
2. Good spotting is essential to the success of this activity. Teach spotting carefully.
3. Do not allow participants to interlock fingers. Interlocking of fingers is likely to cause injury should a participant fall.
4. As partners travel down the Trust V they are more likely to fall. Encourage everyone to simply step forward if they feel like they might fall. Participants can also use the spotters to prevent a fall.

5. When creating the Trust V, it's best to make the sides of the Trust V long (versus short). This will create a *gradual* increase in distance between the partners and this makes the game safer.
6. When participants are traveling down the Trust V, there may come a point where the participants become unsteady. Rather than allowing themselves to fall, encourage participants to simply step forward into the Trust V or brace themselves using the spotters.

Story Line

"You and your partner are traveling through the Amazon jungle and you've come to a river crossing. An unusual two-line bridge has been built across the river. The only way to use the bridge is to cross with a partner. Be careful! There are crocodiles in the river so don't fall in!"

Facilitator Notes

1. The atmosphere in the room during this teambuilding game should be calm and focused.
2. The Trust V activity allows participants to choose the level of challenge they're ready for. When the challenge gets too large, participants simply step forward (into the V, towards their partner) and the challenge is over. For those who want the highest degree of challenge, they can travel all the way to the end of the Trust V.
3. To make it to the end of the Trust V, partners must lean into each other. When they do lean in fully, their bodies are stiff and straight. If partners don't fully trust each other they tend not to lean in fully and instead will bend at the waist which makes it impossible to travel as a team to the end of the Trust V. You might find it necessary to coach the participants to "lean in" and "keep your body straight".

Debriefing Suggestions

The Trust V activity provides a wonderful opening to discuss trust. What is trust? What does trust feel like? Who do you trust? Why do you trust them? To what degree do you trust them?

This activity also provides an opening to discuss commitment. Who / what are you committed to? What does commitment feel like? How do you know when the other person is committed? What would happen if the commitment in our team improved? What would change? What increases a person's ability to commit himself or herself?

Variations

1. Have participants close their eyes while traveling down the Trust V.
2. If the group is large and you have the staff to supervise it, consider creating two Trust Vs so you can have more people actively engaged.

History

A description of this game first appeared in Karl Rohnke's classic teambuilding games book "Cowstails & Cobras II". **www.karlrohnke.com**

Related Quote

"Let this be my last word, that I trust in your love." **~ Rabindranath Tagore**

Turnstile

Group Size: 7 – 20
Age Range: elementary school – adult
Intensity: Mental: easy.........♦................hard
Physical: easy....................♦.....hard
Time: 10 – 20 minutes (without debrief)
Space: minimal..................♦......lots
Set Up Time: 5 minutes
Amount of Duct Tape Required: 60 - 70 feet
View Video: www.DuctTapeTeambuildingGames.com
Username: duct Password: tape

Game Objective

The team must earn as many points as possible in one minute by jumping through the Turnstile.

Skills Developed

Fun, Energizer, Problem Solving, Planning, Goals

Set Up / Preparation

1. Create a 15-feet long section of duct tape "rope". It takes three people to create this duct tape rope: one person who dispenses duct tape and two people to hold the ends of the duct tape. Pull off a 15-feet section of duct tape and have two volunteers hold the ends of this piece of duct tape. Repeat this process three more times, allowing all four long pieces of duct tape to stick to each other. Now have the duct tape holders twist the duct tape rope (the four "strands") - - this will help bind the four 15-feet long strips of duct tape together to make one duct tape rope. If you can, try to string out the 15-feet long strips of duct tape so that their sticky sides are not exposed (this isn't critical). NOTE: This is the same duct tape rope that is used in the games Balance Tug, Stopwatch, Jump Rope Record, Throw Up, and Yurt Circle.
2. Select an appropriate area to play this game. You'll need lots of room and if you play inside you'll need a ceiling that is high enough so that the duct tape rope doesn't hit it when playing.

Presenting the Challenge

1. Gather the group and ask for two volunteers to be jump rope turners. While the rest of the group watches, you will run into the turning jump rope, jump one time and then exit while the jump rope continues to turn. Allow the group members to practice running in and jumping the rope one at a time. After a short practice session read the Presentation Script below.
2. Presentation Script: "Your challenge is to earn as many points as you can in one minute. Your team earns one point each time a team member runs into the turning jump rope, jumps the rope, and then exits successfully." [read the rules below]

Rules

1. If the rope hits the person jumping AND stops, the person jumping does not earn a point for the team and must allow the next person to jump.
2. Participants are allowed to jump the rope multiple times on any given attempt; however, only one point will be earned regardless of the number of jumps. The only way for a person to earn multiple points for the team is to recycle through after other team members have had their turn.
3. If the group sends in 2 people at a time and they can jump the rope and exit successfully, the team earns 2 points. If 3 people jump, the team earns 3 points, and so on.
4. ALL group members must take a turn, including the rope turners. If someone does not want to jump the rope for whatever reason, they must at least walk through.
5. The group must keep track of their own points.

Safety Warning

1. There is a risk of someone tripping on the jump rope and landing hard on the ground.
2. Participants with knee or back problems should not participate in this game.

Story Line

"Your team works for a turnstile manufacturing company and you've just been given the assignment to test the latest and greatest new turnstile design that will be installed in a new state-of-the-art Olympic stadium. Your task is to test the new turnstile to make sure it can handle a very large number of people in a short period of time. Good luck!"

Facilitator Notes

I once worked with the members of a basketball team who earned 152 points in one minute in this game. They played with absolute focus and never allowed the rope to turn without at least two people jumping simultaneously (usually having 3 to 4 people jumping).

Debriefing Suggestions

This is an awesome activity you can use to launch into a discussion about goal setting. After the group establishes an initial record with their first attempt, ask the group to set two goals -- the first goal being a reasonable goal and the second goal being an unreasonable goal. For example, if a group of fifteen people scores 20 points in their first attempt, a reasonable goal might be to earn 40 points in one minute (double the first score). An unreasonable goal might be to earn 60 points (one point for each second).

I point out that unreasonable is not the same as unrealistic. It would be unrealistic for a team to set a goal of earning 20,000 points in one minute if they only earned 20 points with their first attempt. The group will usually beat their reasonable goal but not achieve their unreasonable goal.

I often discuss the attributes of great leaders, such as Martin Luther King Jr. and Gandhi, and ask the group to what degree the rest of the society saw these leaders as being reasonable or unreasonable.

This is not about being unreasonable with other people - it's about being unreasonable with yourself - holding yourself to a higher standard.

I believe it is often the people who are unreasonable in their expectations of themselves who make the greatest positive difference in the world.

Are you being reasonable or unreasonable regarding the expectations you've set for yourself? What areas of your life might you consider for setting some unreasonable standards for yourself?

Variations

1. Set a record and break it.
2. Have the group create a line-up (an order). For each turn of the rope the group must send someone through to jump (not missing a beat of the rope between people). If the rope turns and no one is there to jump, the group must start all over.
3. Allow verbal communication during the planning phase only and no verbal communication during the activity.

History

Karl Rohnke described a variation of this game in his classic teambuilding games book "Silverbullets". **www.karlrohnke.com**

Related Quote

"To do anything truly worth doing, I must not stand back shivering and thinking of the cold and danger, but jump in with gusto and scramble through as well as I can." **~ Og Mandino**

Warp Speed

Group Size: 8 – 15

Age Range: high school – adult

Intensity: Mental: easy..................♦.......hard

Physical: easy....♦.....................hard

Time: 10 – 30 minutes (without debrief)

Space: minimal....... ♦..................lots

Set Up Time: 5 minutes

Amount of Duct Tape Required: 30 - 40 feet

View Video: www.DuctTapeTeambuildingGames.com

Username: duct Password: tape

Game Objective

Pass the four duct tape balls through the established sequence as quickly and efficiently as possible.

Skills Developed

Process Improvement, Problem Solving, Creativity, Planning

Set Up / Preparation

Create four balls out of duct tape. The balls should be about the same size as tennis balls.

Presenting the Challenge

1. The group circles up (include yourself in the circle).
2. Using one of the duct tape balls establish the "official sequence" that will be used throughout the game. To establish this sequence, announce to the group that you need to establish a sequence and to do so you will toss the duct tape ball to someone across the circle. Before throwing the ball, announce this person's name to give them a warning. This person gently tosses the ball to someone else (other than you) across from them. You can only receive and toss the ball one time and you cannot toss it to someone next to yourself. A simple way to keep track of who has yet to receive the ball is to ask everyone to hold their hands out in front of them (catching fashion) and once they catch the ball they are to put their hands by their sides. Once the last person in the group has received the ball, ask them to toss it back to you (this completes the sequence).
3. Make sure the group has the sequence memorized by throwing the ball through the same sequence a second time.
4. Now, take yourself out of the circle and make the person you initially tossed the ball to the first person (I will refer to this person as the Start/Stop Person). The sequence now begins and ends with this person (instead of yourself). Make sure the group understands this. Your job (as the facilitator) now shifts into the role of time keeper.
5. Hand all four duct tape balls to the Start/Stop Person.
6. Now tell the group the following: "Your objective is to pass these four balls through the sequence we just established as quickly and efficiently as possible."

7. You need to be crystal clear about how you tell the group the objective. Each time the group asks you the objective you must repeat it the same way.
8. Allow the group to discuss how they are going to throw the balls quickly if they want to. Otherwise, announce "On your mark, get set, GO!"
9. Time stops once all four tennis balls have made it back into the possession of the Start/Stop Person. Share the time (this new "world record") with the group and ask them if they can beat it. I've never had a group say anything other than "You bet we can!"
10. Allow the group multiple attempts. After each attempt, ask the group if they can beat their previous time (i.e. set a new world record).
11. You can end the activity when the group believes they have the fastest time possible or supply them with a set amount of time to complete the activity (example: "You have five minutes remaining.").

Rules

1. The sequence must remain the same.
2. The sequence must include everyone.
3. All four balls must be passed through the sequence.

Safety Warning

Watch out for participants throwing the duct tape balls too hard because they might hit someone in the eye (that would be bad).

Story Line

"Pass the four hot potatoes through the sequence as fast as you and if you do it fast enough your team can eat them!"

Facilitator Notes

1. This is one of those activities that have a "trick" and if someone in the group knows the trick it can make this activity a non-activity. What is the trick? The fastest way to pass the

4 balls through the sequence is to tape all four balls together (makes them easier to handle) and have the group reconfigure themselves so they are in a circle AND in order. The group can then quickly pass the four balls around the circle (around the sequence), usually under 2 or 3 seconds.

2. The group will undoubtedly figure out that they need to rearrange themselves to speed the passing of the balls. Someone in the group usually asks if this is OK (rearranging the group) - and I respond with “You can do anything you want as long as you don’t break the rules.” It’s not uncommon for a group of 15 to have an initial time of 40 seconds and then, after 8-10 different attempts, to have a final time of 2 or 3 seconds (or lower!).
3. As the facilitator, it’s your job to keep track of the time (each attempt). You can use this data during the debrief session by sharing the attempt number and the score (time) for that attempt. It’s common for a group to experience an initial improvement in time (reduced time) and then hit a barrier where several attempts don’t seem to produce any improved results. Then the group has a breakthrough and is able to further reduce their time. You’ll see this reflected in the data.

The game starts off with the group standing in a circle tossing the balls

Debriefing Suggestions

1. Record the different attempts and the resulting times and share these with the group during the debrief. Ask the group to identify the "shifts" that resulted in a lower time and what brought those shifts about.
2. A "sticking point" your group might wrestle with is the interpretation of the word "pass" when it comes to the stated objective of this activity (as in: "PASS the four balls through the sequence as quickly and efficiently as possible."). Some people will interpret this word to mean "touch" (you must touch the ball) while others will interpret it to mean the ball must simply travel past a team member. I do not interpret the rule for the group even if they ask me for clarification. This allows the group to determine how they want to collectively interpret the rule. When a group wrestles with this issue I always (almost always) bring this up in the debrief. I want to know how and why they came to their decision. I often find that either way the group moves, there is always someone who feels the decision was the wrong way to go and I want to discover how the group feels about (works with) dissent.
3. When the situation is right, I'll ask the group to help me determine when the (low) score is "good enough". Related to this is the issue of "giving up," i.e., when is it time to quit? This can be a very powerful conversation especially if you have strong "Type A" personalities who are never satisfied.
4. This activity provides a great opportunity to see how the group manages creativity and "out of the box" thinking. Is it encouraged? Is it squelched?
5. Ask the group to identify – metaphorically – what the balls represent and what the passing of the balls represents.

Variations

1. Supply the group with a limited period of time to complete the task (example: 20 minutes).
2. Supply the group with a limited number of attempts to get the lowest time possible (example: 10 attempts).

History

This game was taught to me by master teambuilder Betsy Hipple.

Related Quote

"Great teamwork is the only way we create the breakthroughs that define our careers." **~ Pat Riley quotes**

Who Wants The Duct Tape?

Group Size: 10 – 40

Age Range: elementary school – adult

Intensity: <u>Mental</u>: easy...♦......................hard
<u>Physical</u>: easy...♦......................hard

Time: 10 – 15 minutes (without debrief)

Space: minimal............♦.............lots

Set Up Time: 1 minute

Amount of Duct Tape Required: one roll (no pulling off tape)

View Video: www.DuctTapeTeambuildingGames.com
Username: duct Password: tape

Game Objective

Express how much you want the roll of duct tape more than anyone else.

Skills Developed

Fun, Energizer

Set Up / Preparation

Grab one roll of duct tape and you're ready. You don't need to pull any duct tape off the roll.

Presenting the Challenge

1. Circle up the group. Ask everyone to spread out enough so that there's approximately four to six feet distance between participants.
2. The facilitator (you) stand in the center of the circle holding a roll of duct tape. From the center of the circle read the Presentation Script given below.
3. <u>Presentation Script:</u> "This is a simple game to play. In a moment, I'm going to yell out WHO WANTS THE DUCT TAPE?! That is when you are to express how much you want the duct tape. You're allowed to jump up and down, scream and cry, plead madly and do any other antics (within reason) to show me how much you want the duct tape. I will look around the circle for the person who is LEAST expressive in showing how much he or she wants the duct tape. When I find the person who is LEAST expressive I will hand the duct tape over to that person who will take my place at the center of the circle. Once in the center of the circle, that person is the new leader and he/she will lead us all in a quick exercise (like jumping jacks or push ups or dance move, etc.). Then the new leader will yell out WHO WANTS THE DUCT TAPE?! He/she will look for the person who is LEAST expressive in showing how much he or she wants the duct tape - thus starting the cycle all over. We'll play several rounds." [read the rules below]

Rules

During the game, players have to stay in their spot in the circle unless they are picked to be in the center of the circle.

Safety Warning

Some people, when picked to be the leader in the center of the circle, can get carried away with the type of exercises they lead. Let everyone know that if an exercise is too much for them they can alter it to fit their comfort level.

Story Line

"Duct tape is one of the most wonderful things on the face of the planet. One roll of duct tape can cause hysteria in many people. In this game you'll get to experience how most people feel about duct tape."

Facilitator Notes

1. To lead this game well you've got to have a flair for the theatrics. Your energy must be very positive and upbeat because the group will feed off your energy.
2. If the group members are new to each other this game may be hard to lead because participants might not want to look silly in front of each other. If this is the case, try leading some other fun duct tape teambuilding games (example: Hacky Bird, Tail Tag, Pass the Roll) to warm up the group.
3. Play several rounds but be careful about playing the game too long. Pay attention to the group and notice when they start to lose interest in the game (and stop before that!).

Debriefing Suggestions

I typically don't debrief this activity. I tend to focus on simply having fun with this one. If you do want to debrief it, you might ask questions about what it means to be a leader and sharing leadership within the group.

Variations

Require the leader to lead a certain type of exercise - - heart pumping aerobics type, dance moves, Tai Chi moves, etc.

History

This game was taught to me by Gregg Catalano **www.physicansofphun.com**. Gregg uses a rubber chicken for this game instead of a roll of duct tape (isn't that strange?).

Related Quote

"One only needs two tools in life: WD-40 to make things go, and duct tape to make them stop." ~ **G. Weilacher**

Yurt Circle

Group Size: 6 – 12

Age Range: elementary school – adult

Intensity: Mental: easy....♦.....................hard

Physical: easy............♦.............hard

Time: 5 – 10 minutes (without debrief)

Space: minimal...................♦......lots

Set Up Time: 1 minute

Amount of Duct Tape Required: 70 - 80 feet

View Video: www.DuctTapeTeambuildingGames.com

Username: duct Password: tape

Game Objective

The group must create a balanced and stable team circle.

Skills Developed

Fun, Trust

Set Up / Preparation

1. Create a 15-feet long section of duct tape "rope". It takes three people to create this duct tape rope: one person who dispenses duct tape and two people to hold the ends of the duct tape. Pull off a 15-feet section of duct tape and have two volunteers hold the ends of this piece of duct tape. Repeat this process three more times, allowing all four long pieces of duct tape to stick to each other. Now have the duct tape holders twist the duct tape rope (the four "strands") - this will help bind the four 15-feet long strips of duct tape together to make one duct tape rope. If you can, try to string out the 15-feet long strips of duct tape so that their sticky sides are not exposed (this isn't critical). NOTE: This is the same duct tape rope that is used in games such as Balance Tug, Stopwatch, Jump Rope Record, Throw Up, and Turnstile.
2. Join the ends of the duct tape rope. Because the group will be pulling on the duct tape rope circle it is very important to join the ends of the duct tape rope safely and securely. (1) Measure 5 to 6 inches from the end of the duct tape rope and bend (hook) the ends around each other then (2) Tightly wrap several layers of duct tape around the ends to keep them from coming apart. Refer to the photos below:

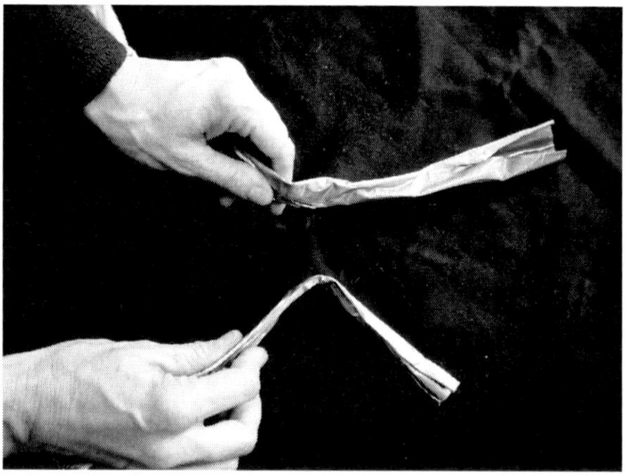

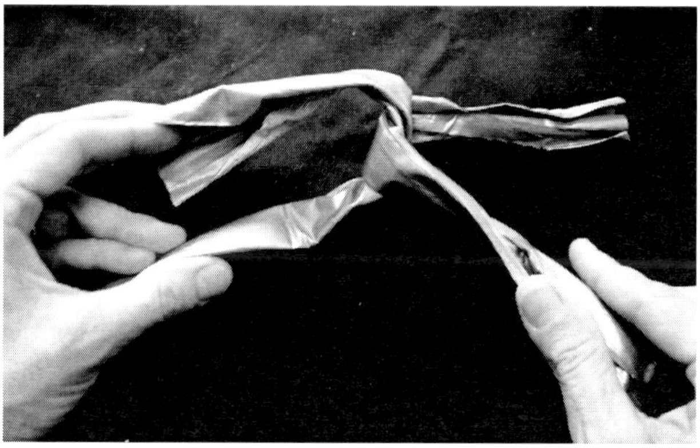

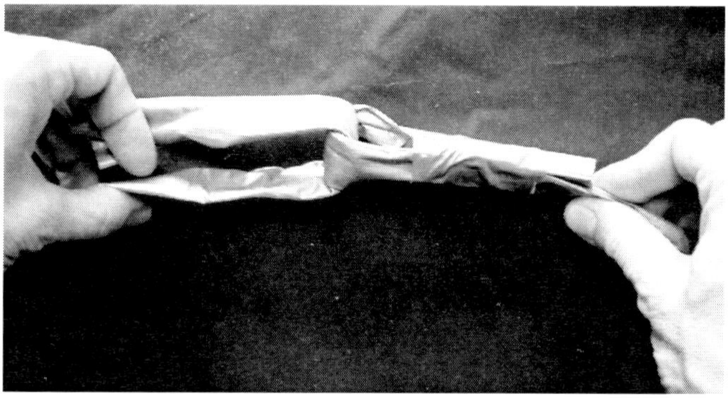

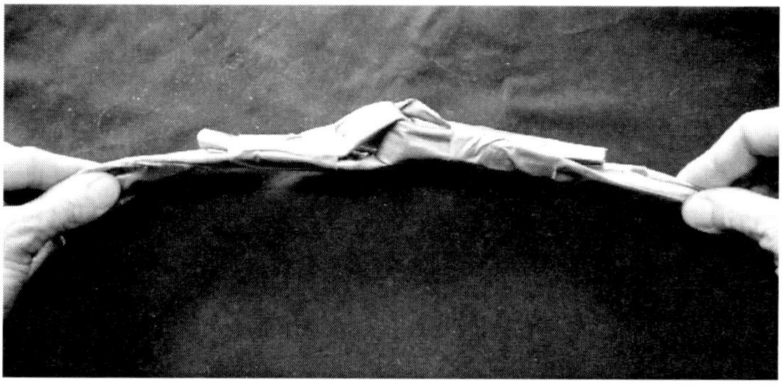

3. Select an appropriate area to play this game. You'll need a flat space large enough for the team to stand in a circle. The surface must not be slippery.

Presenting the Challenge

1. Gather the group into a circle (evenly spaced) and ask everyone to tightly hold onto the duct tape circle with both hands.
2. Presentation Script: "While tightly holding on to the duct tape circle, extend your arms and spread your feet apart to shoulder width. Lean back slightly and begin feeling the tension and support of the circle." [read the rules below]

Rules

1. Participants must remain calm during this activity.
2. Everyone must hold onto the duct tape circle with both hands.

Safety Warning

1. It's extremely important to use high quality duct tape (expensive and thick) for this activity. Using low quality duct tape (inexpensive, thin, and weak) may result in injury. If you are uncertain about the strength of your duct tape and your ability to construct a strong duct tape rope and circle do not lead this activity.
2. This activity will require the group to be calm, responsible and mature. There is a risk that the entire group or a group member could fall down if someone suddenly releases hold on the duct tape circle.
3. Participants with shoulder, back, and knee problems should not participate in this activity.
4. Do not lead this activity on a slippery surface.

Story Line

"You're a group of leaders from around the world who have been brought together at the United Nations to explore and understand the principles required to live in balance and harmony with our planet. To begin this exploration you've been given this Yurt Circle trust exercise to experience and learn from."

Facilitator Notes

1. Make sure you use strong, thick (expensive) duct tape when constructing the duct tape rope and circle.
2. Lead this activity slowly. This activity requires a calm, focusing energy.
3. The group may be reluctant to lean back while holding onto the duct tape circle for fear of the duct tape breaking. If you notice group members are hesitant, ask if they are fearful of the duct tape breaking. If the answer is yes, suggest that everyone sit down on the ground and then pull back on the duct tape circle in an attempt to break it (it's very hard to break). The tentative group members will most probably feel better about trusting the duct tape circle once they experience its strength.

Debriefing Suggestions

I like to use this activity to lead into a discussion about trust. Questions to consider asking the group include:

- Rate the importance of trust on a scale from 1 to 10 with 10 being VERY important.
- Who is ultimately responsible for building trust within the group?
- How does trust affect other aspects of the group (relationships, problem solving, etc.)?
- What is the difference between trusting in oneself and trusting in others? Which is more difficult?
- Has anyone broken your trust and if so, what long term effect did it have on your relationship, if any?
- Are you worthy of someone's trust? (Are you trustworthy?)

Variations

While the group is in balance, ask them to slowly bend their knees and lean back. Each person will end up in a squatting position. Now, return to the standing position. It may be necessary to move people to other parts of the circle to maintain balance. See photo below.

History

This game comes from master teambuilding games leader Karl Rohnke **www.karlrohnke.com**

Related Quote

"The next best thing to being wise oneself is to live in a circle of those who are" ~ **C.S. Lewis**

Appendix

Duct Tape Basics

Duct tape is made by combining the following three layers: 1) sticky rubber based adhesive, 2) strong cloth mesh, and 3) waterproof film.

There are several grades of duct tape and, generally speaking, the most expensive duct tape is the most durable meaning it's stronger (harder to rip) and stickier. Inexpensive duct tape is thinner and rips much easier. The games in this book work best with the more expensive (stronger) duct tape.

Although duct tape is most commonly found in the color grey, it is also available in a wide range of colors including black, white, blue, red, yellow, green, and in many other colors as well.

You can purchase duct tape online and it's commonly found at home improvement stores as well as stores like WalMart.

Find links to all things related to duct tape including videos of each activity in this book by logging onto this book's website:

www.DuctTapeTeambuildingGames.com

Username: duct
Password: tape

"Duct tape is like the force. It has a light side, a dark side, and it holds the universe together."
~ Oprah Winfrey

About The Author

Tom Heck is a professional teamwork coach who helps ordinary people experience extraordinary results when working in teams.

Through his multimedia teambuilding training website TeachMeTeamwork.com, Tom supports the work of over 40,000 team leaders, trainers, facilitators, educators, and coaches in 105 countries.

Tom is the author of multiple team and leadership development training CDs, books and e-books including the most popular teambuilding games e-book ever written entitled Team Activities on a Shoestring which has been downloaded over 50,000 times. He has invented and licensed over 20 team activities that are sold worldwide.

Having received a degree in education from Virginia Tech in 1986, Tom has worked in a variety of positions (government, education, non-profit, for profit) which have provided him with opportunities to help people from a wide range of backgrounds grow and develop as leaders.

Tom's distance learning team & leadership development programs have been attended by leaders from North America, Europe, the Middle East, Africa, the Caribbean, Central & South America, and Asia.

Tom trains, facilitates, and speaks worldwide in a variety of settings. He's worked with groups as small as 5 and as large as 300.

His greatest joy is spending time with his family and enjoying the company of friends. When he's not with family and friends you can find him playing his banjo, building catapults or sailing his catamaran.

Leadership Development Opportunity

Throughout the Duct Tape Teambuilding Games book you've been exposed to activities and ideas designed to help you build high performing teams.

Are you ready for the next step in your leadership evolution? If yes, then I invite you to enroll in the Manager As Coach Boot Camp:

www.ManagerAsCoachBootCamp.com

The Manager As Coach Boot Camp is an intensive VIRTUAL leadership development program for management level staff:

- Delivered LIVE via telephone conference and internet. Fully participate from anywhere in the world; no travel required.
- Leverages the power of a dedicated and focused learning community; learn in the company of like-minded professionals.
- Rigorous. You'll have homework and you'll be held accountable.
- Application oriented. Learning is not enough, you'll be expected to apply what you've learned.
- Professional instruction with personal attention.
- Endorsed by leaders in the training and development industry

In the Manager As Coach Boot Camp, you'll learn proven strategies, tactics and tools for building and leading high performing teams AND you'll receive the ongoing support you need to APPLY what you've learned in street-smart ways.

Finally, and perhaps most importantly, the Manager As Coach Boot Camp will help you become a more conscious leader - - moving out of your head and into your heart.

Manager As Coach Boot Camp has graduates in the United States,, Canada, UK, Ukraine, Saudi Arabia, South Africa, Virgin Islands, and Mexico.

Managers have participated from the business arena, military, healthcare, government, education, and non-profits.

Duct Tape Teambuilding Games Workshop!

Through this book and the accompanying website I've done my best to teach you how to lead Duct Tape Teambuilding Games.

If you're ready to take your Duct Tape Teambuilding Games experience to an even deeper and MORE FUN level, then you're ready for the LIVE workshop based on this book.

- Conferences
- Large group events
- Intact teams
- Train-the-trainer

Experience the joy and exhilaration of the Duct Tape Teambuilding Games as we explore how your group can stick together and become a stronger and more cohesive team!

Teamwork Coach Tom Heck will custom design your event to meet your group's specific training objectives and fun needs.

Contact Tom Heck to learn more:

Tom Heck
Teamwork Coach
tom@tomheck.com
Office: (828) 665-0303

Free Teambuilding Games

Teamwork Coach Tom Heck has created a multimedia website filled with teambuilding resources:

- Free teambuilding ideas e-newsletter
- Free teambuilding games e-book
- Free teambuilding game videos
- Free audio interviews with team & leadership gurus
- Free team and leadership TeleSeminar programs
- Free team theory articles
- And more!

These resources are used by people in 105 countries:

- Trainers
- Coaches
- Facilitators
- Managers & Supervisors
- Teachers
- Team Leaders
- Parents

All of these resources are available to you right now at:

www.TeachMeTeamwork.com

"Tom Heck has created the ultimate resource for anyone who understands the impact of experiential learning and teambuilding. When we hear, we forget. When we see, we're more likely to remember. But when we DO, we understand. There is no better way to engage teachers and learners of all ages than through TeachMeTeamwork.com. As a professional speaker with a passion for teambuilding I am thrilled at the incredible value Tom has built into this powerful resource."
~ Brian Biro
Best selling author and speaker

Multimedia Teambuilding Training CDs from TeachMeTeamwork.com

Now you can own the best selling training tool ever developed by Teamwork Coach Tom Heck of TeachMeTeamwork.com - - it's a virtual train-the-trainer workshop in a 3-CD set filled with over 100 teambuilding games and formatted to teach you fast and easy using video clips, color photos, and printable directions. All at your fingertips, ready to use whenever and wherever you are.

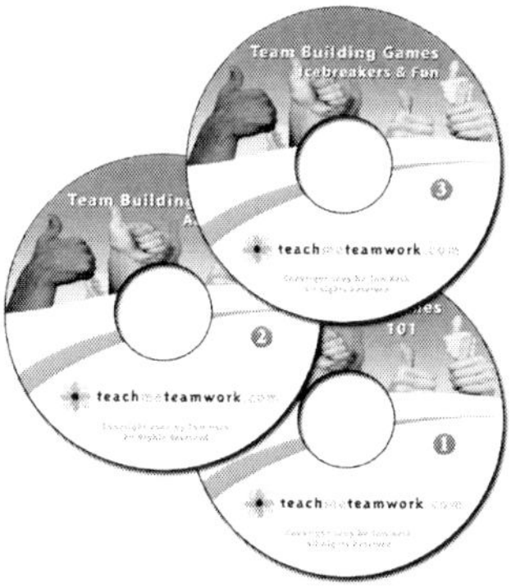

CD # 1
Teambuilding Games 101

CD # 2
Teambuilding Games Advanced

CD # 3
Teambuilding Games Icebreakers and Fun

When you purchase this unique combination of CDs you'll receive a bundle of FREE special bonuses.

Motivate & Inspire Your Team!

Enhance Trust and Build Sustainability!

You can do all of this using the activities found in this best-selling 3-CD Multimedia Teambuilding Games Training set!

Learn more here:

www.TeachMeTeamwork.com

Notes & Ideas

Notes & Ideas

Notes & Ideas

Notes & Ideas